ADRIAN BESLEY

FORCED
LAUGHTER

JOKES FOR ALL RANKS
EVEN ARMCHAIR GENERALS!

Published in 2013 by Prion

an imprint of the Carlton Publishing Group
20 Mortimer Street
London W1T 3JW

10 9 8 7 6 5 4 3 2 1

ISBN 978-1-85375-886-7

A CIP catalogue record of this book can be obtained from the British Library.

Printed and bound in Great Britain by CPI Group (UK) Ltd, Croydon CR0 4YY

ADRIAN BESLEY

FORCED
LAUGHTER

JOKES FOR ALL RANKS
EVEN ARMCHAIR GENERALS!

PRION

INTRODUCTION

There's a really old joke about a boy who writes to his mum after his first week in the army. "Dear Mum," he begins. "Remember all that time you struggled to try to teach me to be polite, to do as I was told, to work hard and help keep the house clean and tidy? Seventeen years and I still never got it. Well guess what? It only took the army three days!"

OK, maybe not the best joke in this book, but it shows why the armed forces are stuffed with jokes. Life in the army, navy or air force runs parallel to civvy life – but living and working in each other's pockets, being subject to intense discipline and having to trust their comrades with their lives has given members of the armed forces a special brand of humour.

So this collection is for those guys – the ones at boot camp getting used to the itchy jumpers and the snoring of the bloke in the next bunk; those out on tour, being woken every morning – not by the alarm radio but by a mortar fire; the guys out at sea trying to remember what other colours there are besides grey; and the RAF pilot wondering if he should have a cappuccino or a latte before morning briefing…

CONTENTS

BASIC
TRAINING

NICKNAMES

The armed forces have their own nicknames for themselves and for each other. Rude, insulting, baffling, they are rarely complimentary! These are just a few of them...

Nickname	Group/Role
The Andrew	The Navy
Bleep/Bunting Tosser	Signalman
Bootnecks	Marines
Brown Jobs	Army squaddies
Bubbleheads	Submarine crew
Chain Gang	Aircraft hands
Commissioned Labourer	Late-entry officer
Crabs	RAF personnel
Crap Hat	Paratroopers' name for anyone not wearing the maroon beret
Crow	Junior soldier
Dabber	Young naval rating
Fish Heads	Navy personnel
Fullscrew	Army corporal
Grunt	Infantryman
Gun-plank	Junior officer (Artillery)
Jimmy the One	First lieutenant (Navy)
Lance Jack/Elsie	Lance corporal (Army)
Lumpy Jumpers	Female service personnel (Army)
Mod Plod	Ministry of Defence guard
NIG	'New In Green' – newcomer (Army)
Penguin	Ground officers with no operational experience (RAF)

Nickname	Group/Role
Percy Pongo	Army personnel
Plonk	Aircraftman second class (the lowest rank in the RAF)
Pusser	Navy personnel
Razz Man	Regimental sergeant major
Rock Apes	RAF personnel
Rodney/Rupert	An officer
Scab Lifter	Medical assistant
Scaleys	Royal Signals personnel
Semi-skimmed	Royal Marines personnel (as green berets look like milk bottle tops)
Shiny-arse	Regimental admin officer
Sky Pilot	Chaplain
Slop Jockey/Cabbage Technician	Chef
Sneaky Beaky	Special Forces personnel
Stab/Weekend Warrior	'Stupid Territorial Army Bastard'
Stripey	Sergeant
Weather Guesser/Professor Fog	Ship's met officer
Wedges	Royal Engineers
Wobbly Orange	Warrant officer
Wooden Tops	Guardsmen

SOME MILITARY SLANG...

The various services, battalions, regiments, even companies
have their own slang – here is a choice selection...

Admin vortex	Disorganized soldier
Ali Baba	Insurgents
Banana boat	Invasion vessel
Beer tokens	Money
Brag rags	Medals
Bumf	Paperwork (from *bum fodder*)
Cake and arse party	Not a good situation
Chicken on a raft	Egg on toast
Chinese wedding cake	Rice pudding
Chin strapped	Knackered
Colonel Gadaffi	The NAAFI
Egg banjo	A fried egg sandwich
Egyptian PT	Sleeping, particularly during the day
Fart sack or green maggot	Sleeping bag
Fat Albert	Hercules cargo aircraft
Flaming onions	An anti-aircraft tracer
Flying a desk	RAF office job
God's Acre	The parade square
Grey Funnel Line	Ships of the Royal Navy
Gucci kit	Non-issued kit or equipment brought by the soldier

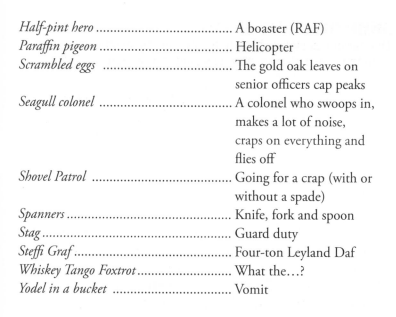

Half-pint hero	A boaster (RAF)
Paraffin pigeon	Helicopter
Scrambled eggs	The gold oak leaves on senior officers cap peaks
Seagull colonel	A colonel who swoops in, makes a lot of noise, craps on everything and flies off
Shovel Patrol	Going for a crap (with or without a spade)
Spanners	Knife, fork and spoon
Stag	Guard duty
Steffi Graf	Four-ton Leyland Daf
Whiskey Tango Foxtrot	What the...?
Yodel in a bucket	Vomit

ACRONYMS

The military seems obsessed with acronyms – so it seems only right that servicemen come up with some of their own...

ARMY	Aren't Ready to be Marines Yet!
BIMBLE	Basic Infantry Manoeuvre But Lacking Enthusiasm – skiving
BOHICA	Bend Over, Here It Comes Again!
CRS	Can't Remember Shit!
CUNT	Civilian Under Naval Training
CYA	Cover Your Arse!
DEH	Don't Expect Help!
DILLIGAF	Does It Look Like I Give a Fuck?
FIDO	Fuck It, Drive On!
FIFO	Fit In or Fuck Off!
FIGMO	Fuck It, Got My Orders!
FILTAB	Fuck It, Let's Take A Break!
FNG	Fuckin' New Guy
FUBAR	Fucked Up Beyond All Repair/Any Recognition
FUBB	Fucked Up Beyond Belief
FUMTU	Fucked Up More Than Usual
TARFU	Things Are Really Fucked Up
FUGAZI	Fucked-Up, Got Ambushed, Zipped-In

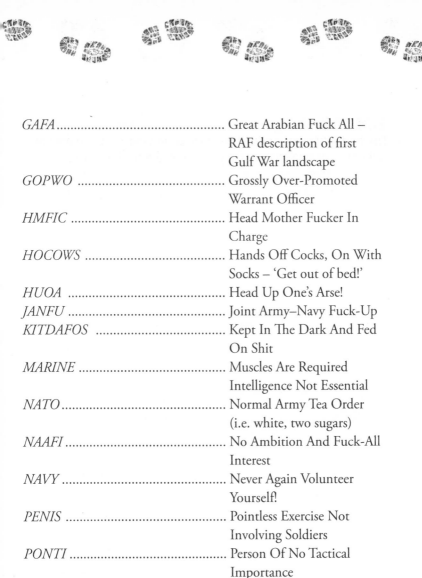

GAFA	Great Arabian Fuck All – RAF description of first Gulf War landscape
GOPWO	Grossly Over-Promoted Warrant Officer
HMFIC	Head Mother Fucker In Charge
HOCOWS	Hands Off Cocks, On With Socks – 'Get out of bed!'
HUOA	Head Up One's Arse!
JANFU	Joint Army–Navy Fuck-Up
KITDAFOS	Kept In The Dark And Fed On Shit
MARINE	Muscles Are Required Intelligence Not Essential
NATO	Normal Army Tea Order (i.e. white, two sugars)
NAAFI	No Ambition And Fuck-All Interest
NAVY	Never Again Volunteer Yourself!
PENIS	Pointless Exercise Not Involving Soldiers
PONTI	Person Of No Tactical Importance
REMF	Rear-Echelon Motherfucker
SHIT	Special High-Intensity Training
SNAFU	Situation Normal: All Fucked Up
SONFI	Switched Off Not Fucking Interested

15

In 2012 it was reported that the MOD had issued a radical new system for assessing prospective recruits. Army careers officers were requested to apply the following procedure and guidelines to determine which area of the forces would best suit each applicant.

Place your prospective recruits alone in a room furnished with only a table and two chairs. Leave them there for two hours without any further instructions. When the time has elapsed, return to the room and assess how they have spent the time.

- If they have disassembled the table, place them with the Royal Engineers.

- If they are counting the number of ceiling tiles, assign them to the Adjutant General's Corps.

- If they are screaming and waving their arms, send them off to the PT Corps.

- If they are talking to the chairs, send them to the Royal Signals Corps.

- If they are sleeping, send them to Sandhurst – they are definitely officer material.

- If they are writing up the experience in an exaggerated fashion, send them to the SAS.

- If they don't even look up when you enter the room, assign them to MOD police.

- If they've drawn an incomprehensible diagram, send them to the Intelligence Corps.

- And, if they try to leave early, direct them to the nearest RAF office.

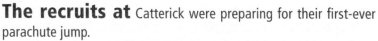

The recruits at Catterick were preparing for their first-ever parachute jump.

The instructors had just demonstrated many of the things that could go wrong. After watching a total malfunction – where the parachute fails to deploy – one of the recruits asked, "Sergeant, if we have a complete malfunction, how much time do we have to deploy our reserve parachutes?"

The sergeant replied, "You have the rest of your life!"

Defence budget cuts forced the training team to start practising mock combat using no explosives, guns, or basically any equipment whatsoever.

In a training scenario, the sergeant in charge tells his recruits that they are under imaginary fire, and to react accordingly.

The recruits scatter. Crouching down behind vehicles, and sheltering in outbuildings, they get into position to return fire. All except for one, who hasn't moved at all.

The sergeant immediately notices this recruit standing out in the open, quite relaxed and unfazed. The sergeant yells at him, "What the devil do you think you're doing? You're under fire!" So the recruit takes one step to the left and, again, remains still.

Now the sergeant is really annoyed. He yells again, "WHAT THE HELL ARE YOU DOING? You're under imaginary fire, take cover!"

The recruit turns to him and replies, "I'm taking cover behind this imaginary tree, Sergeant!"

Young Private Davies had been on the run for a week since going AWOL. He had been sleeping rough and braving the wilds of North Yorkshire. When they finally brought him back again, the sergeant sympathetically asked him why he had decided to leg it from the army.

"Well," replied the young private. "On my first day of basic training, they issued me with a comb, and on that same afternoon the army barber shaved off all my hair.

"On the next day," he continued, "they issued me with a toothbrush, then in the afternoon the army dentist yanked out three of my teeth.

"Well, Sergeant," he went on. "I got up on the third day to find they had given me a jock strap. I wasn't going to hang around until the afternoon."

ARMY RULES FOR NEW RECRUITS:

**If it moves, salute it.
If it doesn't move, pick it up.
If it's too big to pick up, paint it.**

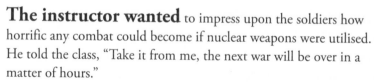

The instructor wanted to impress upon the soldiers how horrific any combat could become if nuclear weapons were utilised. He told the class, "Take it from me, the next war will be over in a matter of hours."

One recruit then blurted, "Result! We'll get the rest of the day off."

The instructor asked the recruit what he would do if he saw a figure crawling toward his position while on guard duty.

"I'd help the officer back to his quarters," was the reply.

A sergeant was passing the recruits' barracks after lights out, when he heard voices from inside. He slammed open the door, and shouted, "Listen, you shower! A few minutes ago, you all heard me say 'good night'. What you have to learn pretty fast, is that you are in the army now. Here 'good night' really means 'shut the fuck up!'"

The room instantly fell silent. But after a few seconds, a small voice could be heard from somewhere in the back of the dark room, "Good night, Sergeant."

At Sandhurst, cadets were taught to remain calm in the event of being captured by the enemy. They should be aware, they were told, that methods used to extract information might not be what they would expect.

"Imagine that the door to your cell opens and in walks a beautiful young woman in a revealing outfit," said the instructor. "The best thing to do is turn away – have nothing to do with her."

From the back of the room came the inevitable question, "Sir, what would be the second best thing?"

The recruits stood at ease as the sergeant announced the day's assignments. He handed out several mundane tasks – sweeping, peeling the spuds etc – and then asked, "Does anyone here have experience with radio communications?"

One enthusiastic young recruit immediately snapped to attention, barely able to contain his excitement, "I do!" he blurted. "I've been an amateur radio enthusiast for many years now."

"Good," replied the sergeant. "You can dig the hole for the new telephone pole."

At Sandhurst the CSM shouted at the officer-cadets, "I will call you 'Sir', and you will call me 'Sir'. The difference is that *you* will mean it!"

Cadets would dread the room inspection. Anything and everything had to be scrubbed, polished and straightened until you could eat your dinner off it. Having not even slept in their beds for fear of creasing their perfect sheets, the cadets of one dorm stood to attention as the officer entered the room.

He checked everything – looking for dust above the window frame and inspecting the lockers.

As he turned to leave, he placed his hand on a laundry bag tied to the end of a bed. There was a crackling sound. "What is in this laundry bag?" he demanded.

"Love letters, sir," answered the nervous cadet.

"What are love letters doing in your laundry bag?" the officer barked.

The cadet quickly answered, "They're pretty dirty, sir!"

The sergeant asks if there are any university graduates among the group of recruits. Several men raise their hands. "Right!" he booms. "You men stand over here." He then turns back to the group and asks for those with college qualifications to take three paces forward.

Then the sergeant says "Right! You recruits with the university educations grab the lawn mowers, you who went to college grab the rakes and the rest of you – watch them – you might learn something."

21

The CSM is briefing the recruits:

"For the next ten weeks the commanding officer will be your father, and I will be your mother. Incidentally, we are not married, so you know what that makes you lot…"

On their first morning of training, the recruits are dragged out of bed by the sergeant and made to assemble outside. "My name is Sergeant Roberts," he snarls. "Is there anyone here who fancies taking me on?"

The soldiers-to-be look stunned as a six-foot-three, 16-stone, muscle-bound recruit raises his hand and says, "Yes, Sergeant, I think I could."

The sergeant approaches the giant and yells, "What's your name recruit?"

"McGraw, Sergeant!"

At this, the sergeant grabs him by the arm and leads him out in front of the group.

"Private McGraw is now my new assistant. Now, is there anyone here who thinks he can take both of us on?"

Sergeant Flint was feared as the toughest instructor in the camp and was determined to let the recruits know it as soon as he started his introductory talk. "You people think you're tough?" he growled. "I'm going to show you what tough really is."

He proceeded to walk to a pond, where he reached in and found a two-foot alligator. He forced open the creature's mouth, stuck in his hand, then placed the alligator on a tree stump. Taking his sidearm from his holster, he deftly reversed it and hit the alligator over the head several times with the butt of the weapon.

The alligator went berserk and closed its savage jaws on Flint's arm. Without even flinching, he hit the beast on the head once more, knocking it out cold, ripped the reptile from his arm and threw it to the ground. He then displayed his torn and bloodied arm without the slightest sign of distress.

"Right, you delicate bunch of mummy's boys," he bellowed, "is there anyone here with the guts to have a go at this?"

From the onlookers came a small, timid voice. "Yes, Sergeant, I would like to try."

"Are you sure you can handle it?" asked the amazed instructor.

More confidently the recruit replied, "Well, as long as you promise you won't hit me on the head as hard as you hit the alligator."

One day on a SERE (Survival, Evasion, Resistance, Extraction) training camp, an instructor caught up with a group on a survival expedition. As they patiently sat round a large pot boiling on the fire, he asked, "So, what's on the menu tonight?"

One soldier said he had added a squirrel to the pot, another mentioned the handful of mushrooms he had put in, a third mentioned a rat, while another said he had collected a pound of grubs, and so on. "Great work, men," said the instructor as he sniffed the pot and he left them to their supper.

An hour later he returned and noticed that all the men were still sitting round the pot. None of them appeared to have eaten. Puzzled, he asked the men if they were hungry.

"Yes, sir, we're starving!" the soldiers answered.

"Well, why don't you tuck in, then?" asked the instructor.

"We're waiting until it's too dark to see what it looks like, sir!"

An instructor was trying to teach Private Johnson, a new and not-too-bright soldier, how to navigate by finding the North Star. The instructor did his best, but he could see that it wasn't getting through, so he just hoped no one would test the private on it.

A couple of weeks later, during a long march by night, the Sergeant halted the platoon and asked, "Private Johnson, quickly, where's the North Star?"

Private Johnson looked hard at the sky for a long time, then confidently declared, "We've already passed it, Sergeant!"

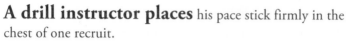

A drill instructor places his pace stick firmly in the chest of one recruit.

"Private," he bawls. "There's a piece of shit on the end of this stick!"

Quick as a flash came the reply. "Yes, Sergeant, but which end?"

A career army officer was jump master for his unit and was taking a few novices up for a drop. The flight was pretty rough, and, after a while, he called off the jump because of high winds. As the plane headed back to base the pilot pulled off an extremely smooth landing, but two of the trainees started throwing up.

"How come you could take that rough flight but you get airsick on such a smooth landing?" asked the seasoned para.

"Well, sir," one trainee explained. "We've always jumped out of planes. We've never actually landed before."

To all trained Territorial Army personnel:

Under the Emergency Powers Act (1939) as amended by the Defence Act (1978), you are hereby notified that you are required to place yourself on standby for possible military service in Afghanistan.

You may shortly be ordered to depart for wherever the godforsaken place might be, where you will join either the 3rd Battalion of the Queen's Own Suicidals or the 2nd Foot and Mouth. Unfortunately the regular army is too busy helping out with the Olympics to be there themselves.

Due to the recent rundown of the navy and the refusal of P&O to lend us any of their liners, it will be necessary for you to make your own way to the combat zone. HM Government has been able to negotiate a 20% discount on trips to Afghanistan with Virgin Airlines and you are strongly advised to take advantage of this offer (Ryanair offer a £39.99 one-way trip to an airport only 12 hours away by camel and the easyJet fare is only £12.99, but you will be surcharged for any oxygen you breathe in after take-off).

Because of cutbacks in government expenditure, it will be advisable for you to equip yourself with the following:

- As many Pot Noodle cartons as you can carry
- Combat trousers (preferably khaki)
- Helmet (cycling or hard-hats are acceptable)
- A video camera for making amusing fly-on-the-wall videos of fellow soldiers
- Incontinence pads
- Gas mask or canary
- Map of the combat zone (OS 1:2800 leisure map of Helmand Province is suitable)
- Travel Scrabble
- Condoms
- Suntan oil

If you are in a position to afford it, we would like you to purchase a tank (Vickers Defence of Banbury are currently offering all new conscripts a 0% finance deal on all Y registration Chieftains, but hurry, as this offer is only available while stocks last).

We should like to reassure you that in the unlikely event of anything going wrong, you will receive a free burial in the graveyard of your choice, and your next of kin will be entitled to the new War Pension of £3.75 per calendar month, index-linked but subject to means testing, and fully repayable should our side eventually lose.

There may be little time for formal military training before your departure and so we advise that you should hire videos of the following films and try to pick up as many tips as you can whilst you watch them:

- The Guns of Navarone
- Lawrence of Arabia
- Kelly's Heroes
- A Bridge Too Far
- Dumb and Dumber
- Apocalypse Now
- Forrest Gump
- Team America: World Police

Yours faithfully

Whatever Old Etonian is currently running
the Ministry of Defence

OPENING HOSTILITIES

Whilst ferrying marines back and forth from an operation, a helicopter lost power and went down. Skilfully the pilot managed to bring the craft down safely, landing in the sea.

Struggling to get out, one marine tore off his seat belt, inflated his life vest and jerked open the exit door.

"Don't panic!" yelled the pilot. "This thing is designed to float!"

As the marine leapt into the sea, he yelled back, "Yeah, well, it was also supposedly designed to FLY!"

After being transferred to a new barracks, a young soldier called to tell his wife that his leave had been cancelled. "They found some dirty magazines," he said, "and the whole company is being disciplined."

"That's ridiculous," his wife contended. "These are grown men, many away from their wives and girlfriends for long periods of time. People expect them to go without basic pleasures even though they are willing to put their lives on the line. And they are being penalized for something so trivial, this kind of freedom is what they are supposed to be defending…"

Eventually her husband managed to get a word in edgeways. "Babe, when I said 'dirty magazines', I meant the clips from their rifles hadn't been cleaned."

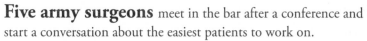

Five army surgeons meet in the bar after a conference and start a conversation about the easiest patients to work on.

"I prefer to work on stackers because everything inside is numbered and listed in order," said the first.

The second retorted, "Signalmen are easier because everything is tie-wrapped in bundles and colour coded."

A third opined, "Shinys are pretty easy because everything is classified to a decimal point and there is an index."

And a fourth volunteered, "I like squaddies because they are rough and ready and they don't get picky if you put it all back together with a few parts left over."

Finally, one surgeon who had stayed silent, stood up and announced, "I have to say I most like to work on officers because they have no balls, no brains, no backbone and the head and the arse are interchangeable!"

In the local bar a soldier was bragging about how he severed a man's arm with his bayonet.

One of the locals looked quizzically at him and asked, "Shouldn't you have severed his head instead?"

At this the soldier's mate butted in, "Nah, his head was already severed."

The army were looking for a cold, clinical killer for a covert operation. After completing all the background checks interviews, and testing, there were just three candidates: two men and a woman.

For the final test, the recruitment officer took one of the men to a thick metal door and handed him a gun.

"We must be certain that you will follow instructions without hesitation. Inside this room, you will find your wife sitting in a chair. You must kill her immediately."

The candidate replied, "You can't be serious. I won't shoot my wife!"

The officer shook his head. "Then you're not the right man for this job. Take your wife and go home."

The second man was given the same instructions. He took the gun and went into the room. All was quiet for five minutes. Then he came out with tears in his eyes. "I tried, but I can't kill my wife."

The recruiter said, "You don't have what it takes for this mission. Take your wife and go home."

Finally, it was the woman's turn. She was given the same instructions, to kill her husband. She took the gun and went into the room. Several shots were heard, followed by screaming, crashing and banging on the walls. After a minute of mayhem, there was total silence. Then the door opened slowly and the woman came out, wiping sweat from her brow.

"The gun was loaded with blanks," she said, "so I had to beat him to death with the chair."

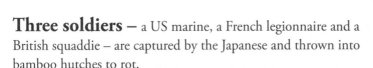

Three soldiers – a US marine, a French legionnaire and a British squaddie – are captured by the Japanese and thrown into bamboo hutches to rot.

Some months later the camp commandant decides to have some fun. He gives each of the three prisoners two steel balls and tells them that whoever comes up with a clever idea for the balls will be released.

The next morning he visits the prisoners. The legionnaire has woven a cradle out of grass for the balls and made an executive toy. The commandant is impressed and sets him free.

In the next hutch the marine is sitting cross-legged, meditating and the two steel balls are levitating two feet off the ground. Again the commandant is impressed and releases the prisoner.

Finally he moves to the British squaddie's hutch. He is smoking a fag and scratching his arse with no sign of the steel balls. The commandant is furious and asks him what he has done with them.

The squaddie shrugs. "Dunno. I lost one and broke the other."

The unit engineer had just finished a talk on the advantages of mechanization and how much work could now be carried out by machines. One officer was left deep in thought.

"Got you thinking did it, Captain?" asked the major.

"Ah, yes! I just thought of something myself that could do the work of fifty men," replied the captain.

"I'm intrigued," replied the major. "What did you have in mind?"

"Two hundred soldiers!" was the reply.

IN THE

ARMY NOW

"Can you tell me the difference between valour and discretion?" asked the Sergeant.

Private Stevens replied: "Well, leaving one's barracks without permission would be valour."

"And discretion?"

"Not going back again?"

'Troops are warned not to drink any water which has not been passed by the Medical Officer.'

A warrant officer walks into a brothel and asks the madam, "How much would it be for the pleasure of my company this evening?"

Madam looks him up and down and replies, "Fifty quid."

"Fifty quid?" replies the WO. "That's very reasonable… COMPANY… QUICK MARCH… left, right, left, right…"

Bomb Disposal Squad T-shirt slogan:

'If I'm running, try to keep up.'

Lieutenant Smith was trying to get a can of cola from the vending machine but didn't have the right change. He saw Private Jones mopping the floor and asked him, "Do you have change for a pound Private?"

Private Jones replied, "Sure. No problem," and reached into his pocket.

The lieutenant was furious. "That's no way to address a superior officer! Now let's try it again. Private, do you have change for a pound?"

Private Jones replied, "No, SIR! I haven't."

"Hurry up, Private, my dead mother could dig a hole faster than you!" barked the sergeant.

"Yeah, that's because she's got a six-foot start on me!" came the reply.

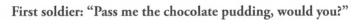

First soldier: "Pass me the chocolate pudding, would you?"

Second soldier: "No way!"

First soldier: "Why ever not?"

Second soldier: "It's against regulations to help another soldier to dessert!"

Q. What's the second most dangerous thing in the British Army?

A. An officer with a map...

Q. And the most dangerous?

A. Two officers sharing the same map.

Private: "Sir? If I said you were an idiot, what would you do?"

Officer: "I would have you court-martialled for insubordination."

Private: "Sir? If I only *thought* you were an idiot, what would you do?"

Officer: "Well, I couldn't do much about that."

Private: "Sir? I think you're an idiot."

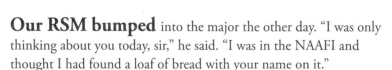

Our RSM bumped into the major the other day. "I was only thinking about you today, sir," he said. "I was in the NAAFI and thought I had found a loaf of bread with your name on it."

"Oh, yes?" smiled the puzzled major, wondering where this was going.

"Yeah, then I realized it actually said 'Thick Cut', sir!"

The CO noticed that one of his men was behaving oddly. The soldier would pick up any piece of paper, break into tears and say, "That's not it."

This went on for some time, until the officer arranged to have the soldier examined.

A military psychiatrist concluded that the soldier was suffering from a mental disorder and was unfit for service. The shrink wrote out his discharge paper and handed it to the soldier, who smiled and said, "That's it."

During a kit inspection, the sergeant said, "The amount of stuff that goes into a soldier's kit bag is positively staggering."

A soldier commented, "So is the bloke underneath it."

A radio operator saw a shape moving towards him through the bush. He opened fire and was relieved to hear a shriek as the enemy went down. Moving in to investigate, he found his platoon sergeant on his back with glazed eyes and blood pumping from a gaping hole in his chest.

He immediately radioed through to HQ. "Somebody help!" he yelled in a panic. "I think my sergeant is dead. What should I do?"

A reassuring voice on the other end replied, "Stay calm, soldier. First, you need to check that he's actually dead. He might have just lost consciousness."

There was a silence, then the sound of a single shot.

The soldier came back to the radio, "OK, so now what?"

"Dear Dad," read the young soldier's first letter home. "I cannot tell you where I am, but yesterday I shot a polar bear…"

Several months later came another letter. "Dear Dad, I still cannot tell you where I am, but yesterday I danced with a hula girl…"

Two weeks later came yet another note. "Dear Dad, I still cannot tell you where I am, but yesterday the doctor told me I should have danced with the polar bear and shot the hula girl."

A young private never quite got over his miserable poverty-stricken childhood. He joined the army on turning 18, but old habits die hard, and one night the duty sergeant found him rummaging through the garbage and eating out of discarded cans and jars.

"On your feet, Private!" he bellowed. "You're no better than the rest of us! You'll eat in the NAAFI like we have to!"

Normal people believe that 'if it ain't broke, don't fix it'.

Sergeant majors believe that if it ain't broke, it doesn't have enough features yet.

A sergeant in a parachute regiment took part in several night-time exercises. Once, he was seated next to a lieutenant fresh from Jump School. He looked a little pale, so the sergeant struck up a conversation.

"Scared, sir?" he asked.

"No, just apprehensive," the lieutenant replied.

The sergeant grunted, "What's the difference?"

"It means I am scared, but I have a university education."

COLONEL'S DIRECTIVE TO HIS EXECUTIVE OFFICERS:

"Tomorrow evening at approximately 20:00 hours, Halley's Comet will be visible in this area; an event which occurs only once every 75 years. Have the men fall out in the battalion area in fatigues, and I will explain this rare phenomenon to them. In case of rain, we will not be able to see anything, so assemble the men in the theatre and I will show them films of it."

EXECUTIVE OFFICER TO COMPANY COMMANDER:

"By order of the Colonel, tomorrow at 20:00 hours, Halley's Comet will appear above the battalion area. If it rains, fall the men out in fatigues, then march to the theatre where this rare phenomenon will take place, something which occurs only once every 75 years."

COMPANY COMMANDER TO LIEUTENANT:

"By order of the Colonel, be in fatigues at 20:00 hours tomorrow. The phenomenal Halley's Comet will appear in the theatre. In case of rain in the battalion area, the Colonel will give another order, something which occurs once every 75 years."

LIEUTENANT TO SERGEANT:

"Tomorrow at 20:00 hours, the Colonel will appear in the theatre with Halley's Comet, something which happens every 75 years. If it rains, the Colonel will order the comet into the battalion area."

SERGEANT TO SQUAD:

"When it rains tomorrow at 20:00 hours, the phenomenal 75-year-old General Halley, accompanied by the Colonel, will drive his comet through the battalion area theatre in fatigues."

Two privates had almost dug their trench to regulation depth. They turned to see a full screw manically digging so deep that only his shovel tip was visible from the hole.

When their sergeant passed by, one spoke up. "Sergeant, do you know what's wrong with the corporal? He seems to have gotten a little carried away."

"Oh, he'll be all right," the sergeant replied. "He suffers from Corporal Tunnel Syndrome."

To the optimist, the glass is half full. To the pessimist, the glass is half empty. To the sergeant major, the glass is twice as big as it needs to be.

RULES OF THE RUCKSACK:

1. No matter how carefully you pack, the rucksack is always too small

2. No matter how small, the rucksack is always too heavy

3. No matter how heavy, the rucksack will never contain what you want

4. No matter what you need, it's always at the bottom.

Joe Simpson enlisted in the army. Flown out to Iraq, he became Private Simpson. The next day, he learned that his best friend had moved his wedding to the coming weekend, so he asked his commanding officer for a three-day pass.

"Are you serious?" the CO replied. "You just got here and you already want a three-day pass? You are going to have to do something pretty fucking spectacular to get one of those!"

Later that day, Private Simpson came back driving an Iraqi tank. The CO ran out to greet him. "I can't believe it!" he said. "You've captured an Iraqi tank! How did you do it?"

"Let's just say I used what I got up here," the private answered, tapping the side of his head.

"Fair enough," the CO said. "Well done, Private. You've certainly earned your three-day pass!"

The CO happily jumped into the tank and drove it to headquarters. Private Simpson started towards his barracks.

"Joe! Wait up!" one of his mates called as he caught up with him. "How did you do it?"

Private Simpson looked around and then answered, "It was like this. I jumped in a tank and drove it out of town. I spotted an Iraqi tank, so I popped my head out and raised a white flag to get his attention. When the raghead popped his head out of his tank, I said, 'Hey! Do you want to get a three-day pass?' He said, 'Yes!' I said, 'Me too!' So we switched tanks!"

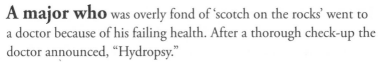

A major who was overly fond of 'scotch on the rocks' went to a doctor because of his failing health. After a thorough check-up the doctor announced, "Hydropsy."

"And what is Hydropsy?" asked the major.

The doctor answered, "There is more water in your body than is good for you."

The major exclaimed, "My dear doctor, I'll have you know that I never drink water." Then, as an afterthought, he added, "It must have been all that ice."

A new soldier was on sentry duty at the main gate. His orders were clear: no car was to enter unless it had a special sticker on the windshield. A big car came up with a general seated in the back. The sentry said, "Halt, who goes there?"

The chauffeur – a corporal – replied, "General Dorkin-Jones."

"I'm sorry, I can't let you through," said the new soldier. "You've got to have a sticker on the windshield."

The General said irritably to the driver, "Drive on, Corporal!"

The sentry said, "Hold on! You really can't come through. I have orders to shoot if you try driving in without a sticker."

The general repeated to the driver, "Corporal, drive on! That's an order!"

The sentry walked up to the rear window and said, "General, I'm pretty new at this. Do I shoot you or the driver?"

After a recent war, a British regiment commander was addressing some troops under his command who had heroically performed above and beyond the call of duty. He informed them that Her Majesty's Army had committed to reward each of the three soldiers £100 per inch of distance between two different parts of the man's body.

The CO asked, "Where would you like to be measured, Sergeant?"

"From the top of my head to the soles of me feet, sir!" the Sergeant replied.

"Very good!" the CO said, and the sergeant was measured at six-foot-five. He was paid the handsome sum of seven thousand pounds.

A second soldier was asked, "What about you, Corporal?"

"Between the tips of the fingers of my outstretched arms, sir!" the corporal said.

"Very good!" replied the CO. The Corporal, a man of considerable wingspan, was rewarded with eight thousand quid.

Finally, the last soldier was addressed. "And you, Private, where would you like measured?"

"From the tip of me penis to the base of me balls, sir!" said the private.

The CO replied, "I must admit this is quite an unusual request, Private, but it's your decision." He ordered the private to drop his pants for the ensuing measurement. Immediately the CO's mouth fell agape and he stammered, "Where in God's name are your gonads, Private?"

The private proclaimed, "Helmand Province, Afghanistan, sir!"

During an army training exercise the commanding officer's jeep got stuck in the mud. The CO saw some men lounging around nearby and asked them to help him get unstuck.

"Sorry, sir," said one of the loafers, "but we've been classified dead and the umpire said that we can't contribute in any way."

The CO turned to his driver and said, "Go drag a couple of those dead bodies over here and throw them under the wheels to give us some traction."

A woman visits the doctor to complain that she was no longer getting any satisfaction from sex with her husband. "How long has this problem lasted?" asked the doc.

"Let me see. It was fine when he was in the Guards," she replied. "But it started going wrong last year when he was given his place in the SAS."

"Ah!" exclaimed the doctor. "That'll be the problem. The SAS train their men to get in and out without anyone noticing."

Two goldfish are in a tank. One turns to the other and says, "How the fuck do you drive this thing?"

THE FIVE RESPONSES OF THE QUARTERMASTER:

1. Nope. We ain't got it.

2. You're not authorized for one.

3. If I give you one, I'll have to give one to everybody else.

4. If I give you one, there'll be none left on the shelf.

5. We'll give you a new one when you've brought the old one back.

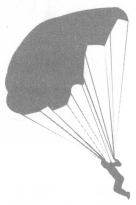

A young soldier was making his first parachute jump. The corporal explained the procedure. "You count to ten and pull the first ripcord. If the chute doesn't open, pull the second. That should do it. Then, after you land, there'll be a truck waiting to pick you up."

The soldier checked his gear, called out "Geronimo!" and jumped out of the plane. He counted to ten and pulled the ripcord. The chute failed to open. He pulled the second ripcord and the chute still didn't open. As he plummeted downwards, he said, "Knowing my luck, that bleeding truck won't be there either!"

An architect, an artist and a sergeant major were discussing whether it was better to spend time with the wife or a mistress. The architect said he enjoyed time with his wife, building a solid foundation for an enduring relationship. The artist said he enjoyed time with his mistress, because of the passion and mystery he found there.

The sergeant major said, "I like both."

"Both?" the others replied.

"Yeah. If you have a wife and a mistress, they'll both assume you're are spending time with the other woman, so you can stay out and get some work done."

THE TWO RULES OF THE ARMY:

RULE 1: The Commanding Officer is always right.

RULE 2: If the Commanding Officer is not right, see Rule 1.

In the midst of a blazing battle, the captain shouted an order to a nearby soldier. Without hesitation, the soldier ran across the battlefield, dodging a hail of enemy fire, to retrieve a dispatch case from a dead soldier and then dived back to safety.

"Private," said the captain, "I'm recommending you for a medal. You risked your life to save the location of our secret warehouses."

"Warehouses?" the Private shouted. "I thought you said 'whorehouses'!"

An army sergeant major walks into a brothel. The madam takes him upstairs and picks out the best girl they have. The sergeant major immediately disrobes and stands with his hands on his hips. "My name is Sergeant Major Jones, I've been in the army thirty years, and I'm the master of my mind and body, 'DICK, ATTEN-SHUN!'"

Immediately, his penis becomes fully erect. The prostitute is in awe and asks him how he can do that. The sergeant major replies, "Like I said, I've been in the army thirty years, and I'm a master of my mind and body, 'DICK, AT EASE!'"

His manhood immediately goes limp. The prostitute still can't get over the display and asks him for another demonstration. The sergeant major says, "I'm the master of my mind and body, 'DICK, ATTEN-SHUN!'" – which produces a raging hard-on once again. He follows this display with the command, "DICK, AT EASE!" and his member goes limp once again.

The prostitute still can't believe her eyes and asks for the demonstration one more time. The sergeant major shouts, "I've been in the army thirty years, and I'm the master of my mind and body, 'DICK, ATTEN-SHUN!'"

His ol' fella becomes immediately erect, and then he gives the command, "DICK, AT EASE!"

The Sergeant Major looks down but, to his amazement, his penis is still hard.

"Apparently you didn't hear me, soldier. I said 'DICK, AT EASE!'" But his penis is still fully erect. The sergeant major is now fuming, and says, "I'm going to tell you one more time, 'DICK, AT EASE!'"

No luck. His penis is still rock hard. He yells, "Right! You were warned!" moves to the side of the bed and starts to rub his member vigorously.

The prostitute asks, "What the hell is going on?"

The sergeant major replies, "This soldier disobeyed a direct order, and I'm giving him a dishonourable discharge!"

The first female army recruit reported for duty and was told that although her quarters would be in a separate building, she was to mess with the men.

It wasn't until four weeks later that someone finally told her that this meant to eat her meals with them.

The weekly training schedule had been posted on the notice board. Once again the rifle range session had been cancelled; however, an extra cross-country run had been substituted.

"Does it bother anyone else," asked one soldier, "that the army doesn't seem concerned with how well we can shoot, yet seems extremely bothered by how fast we can run?"

I was working in the mess hall of my army base, and my commanding officer walked up to me.

"I'll have a cheeseburger and fries," he said.

I replied, "Is that an order?"

The men had been in the field for four weeks straight. The platoon sergeant called them together and said, "First the bad news: we have to stay out another two weeks."

The soldiers collectively replied, "Aww."

"Now the good news: you're getting a change of underwear."

The men all cheered.

The sergeant then said, "OK. 1st Squad change with 2nd Squad, 3rd Squad change with 4th Squad!"

ADJUTANT GENERAL'S CORPS' SOP:

If it rings, put it on hold.

If it beeps, call a tech.

If it whistles, ignore it.

If it's a friend, go for a smoke.

If it's the CO, look busy.

If it talks, take notes.

If it's handwritten, type it.

If it's typed, copy it.

If it's copied, file it.

If it's Friday, FORGET IT!

Back at base after a combined arms exercise, I noticed all the paras wearing T-shirts emblazoned with 'Death From Above!' Later I saw some submariners whose T-shirts declared 'Death From Below!'

Then, standing in line for scran, I was served by an army cook. His T-shirt promised: 'Death From Within!'

If at first you don't succeed... Bomb Disposal is probably not for you...

While the soldiers stood at attention during a parade, a private waved to someone in the crowd.

"Private, eyes front and NEVER do that again!" the drill sergeant whispered menacingly. But a few minutes later, the soldier waved a second time.

Back in barracks after the parade, the sergeant stormed in and barked for the private to step forward. "You're in deep shit, Private! What's wrong with you? Aren't you afraid of me?"

"Yes, Sergeant!" replied the private. "But I'm even more scared of my mother!"

SAIL THE

SEVEN SEAS

***HMS Albion* pulled** into Yokosuka, Japan, for a port call. "Men," the lieutenant addressed his troops, "I want you to experience the local culture. Don't eat things that you can get at home. For God's sake, sample some Japanese food!"

At the end of the visit, the officer approached a private from Scotland. "McLean," he asked. "What did you eat that was different, Private?"

"I had a burger, sir."

"A burger? Are you telling me you can't get a burger in Glasgow?"

"Oh, of course, sir," McLean replied, "This was a Japanese burger – It had soy sauce on it."

THE FIVE MOST DANGEROUS THINGS IN THE ROYAL NAVY:

1. A seaman saying, "I learned this at BRNC…"

2. A petty officer saying, "Trust me, sir…"

3. A lieutenant JG saying, "Based on my experience…"

4. A lieutenant saying, "I was just thinking…"

5. A commander chuckling and saying, "Watch this shit…"

A second lieutenant on sea duty overheard a recruit saying he was going downstairs. "Listen, Sailor," he snarled, "Downstairs is 'below', that side is 'starboard', up there is 'aft' and over there is 'port side'. Now if I ever hear you say one more civvy word like 'downstairs' again, I'll throw you through that little round window over there!"

The US and British Navies were recently on manoeuvres in the Persian Gulf. The communications officer aboard the aircraft carrier *USS Enterprise* sent a radio message to the British carrier *HMS Illustrious*:

"And how is the second biggest navy in the world today, then?"

To which the *Illustrious* officer responded, "Fine. How's the second best?"

Once upon a time there was a famous commander in the Royal Navy. He had captained the great ships of the fleet, led many successful operations and had been highly decorated. However, there was one thing different about this captain. Every morning he went through a strange ritual. He would lock himself in his quarters and open a small safe. In the safe was an envelope with a piece of paper inside. He would stare at the paper for a minute, and then lock it back up. Afterwards he went about his daily duties.

For years this went on, and his crew became very curious. Was it an inspirational poem? Could it be a letter from a long-lost love? Or was it a list of colleagues lost in battle that drove him to his great deeds? Everyone speculated about the contents of the strange envelope.

Then, one day, the captain died at sea. After laying the captain's body to rest, the first mate and some others entered the captain's quarters. The first mate opened the safe, retrieved the envelope, opened it and then turned pale while showing the paper to the others. Four words were on the paper:

Port = Left, Starboard = Right

In light of the latest defence budget cuts, the navy has announced a more up-to-date recruitment campaign:

'The Royal Navy: We're all in the same boat.'

There are two kinds of naval vessels: submarines and targets.

A young officer cadet was assigned to the submarine service, where he had dreamed of working ever since he was small boy. He tried to impress the petty officer with the expertise he had picked up at Britannia Royal Naval College.

The petty officer cut him off quickly by saying, "Listen, sir, it's really simple. Add the number of times we dive to the number of times we surface. Divide that number by two. If the result doesn't come out as even, don't open the hatch."

Transcript of a radio conversation between a
US naval ship and Canadian authorities off the
coast of Newfoundland in October 1995

Canadians: Please divert your course 15 degrees to the South
to avoid a collision. Over.

Americans: Recommend you divert *your* course 15 degrees to
the North to avoid a collision. Over.

Canadians: Negative. You will have to divert your course 15
degrees to the South to avoid a collision. Over.

Americans: This is the Captain of a US Navy ship. I say
again, divert *your* course. Over.

Canadians: No. I say again, you divert *YOUR* course. Over.

Americans: THIS IS THE AIRCRAFT CARRIER
USS *LINCOLN*, THE SECOND LARGEST SHIP IN
THE UNITED STATES' ATLANTIC FLEET. WE
ARE ACCOMPANIED BY THREE DESTROYERS,
THREE CRUISERS AND NUMEROUS SUPPORT
VESSELS. I DEMAND THAT YOU CHANGE YOUR
COURSE 15 DEGREES NORTH, I SAY AGAIN,
THAT'S ONE FIVE DEGREES NORTH, OR
COUNTERMEASURES WILL BE UNDERTAKEN
TO ENSURE THE SAFETY OF THIS SHIP. OVER.

Canadians: This is a lighthouse. Your call. Over.

TAKEN FROM ROYAL NAVY AND MARINES APPLICANTS' OFFICER FITNESS REPORTS:

- His men would follow him anywhere, but only out of curiosity.

- I would not breed with this officer.

- This officer is not so much of a has-been, but more of a definitely won't-be.

- When she opens her mouth, it is only to change whichever foot was previously in there.

- He has carried out each and every one of his duties to his entire satisfaction.

- He would be out of his depth in a car-park puddle.

- Technically sound, but socially impossible.

- This officer reminds me very much of a gyroscope – always spinning around at a frantic pace, but not really going anywhere.

- This young lady has delusions of adequacy.

- When he joined my ship, this officer was something of a granny. Since then, he has aged considerably.

- This officer has used my ship to carry his genitals from port to port, and my officers to carry him from bar to bar.

- Since my last report he has reached rock bottom, and has started to dig.

- She sets low personal standards and then consistently fails to achieve them.

- He has the wisdom of youth, and the energy of old age.

- This officer should go far – and the sooner he starts, the better.

- In my opinion this pilot should not be authorized to fly below 250 feet.

- The only ship I would recommend this man for is citizenship.

- Works well when under constant supervision and cornered like a rat in a trap.

- This man is depriving a village somewhere of an idiot.

- Only occasionally wets himself under pressure.

One day, two ratings and their petty officer are setting off on shore leave. Suddenly, one rating sees something shiny floating in the water. He reaches down to retrieve it and finds it is an old lamp. Eager to see if it is worth anything, he rubs it dry, and as he does so, a genie pops out of the lamp and says, "I am the Genie of the Lamp and I grant each one of you one wish."

The rating says, "I found it so I should go first." He thinks for a few seconds before saying, "My wish is that I will never want for money for the rest of my life."

Pfffff! In a burst of smoke he disappears.

The other rating goes next. He has already prepared his wish. "I'd like to live in a tropical paradise and have beautiful young women wait on my every need."

Pfffff! Off he went to have his dreams fulfilled.

The genie now turns to the officer. "What can I grant you with your dashing uniform and straight back?" he asks, without a touch of irony. The PO looks him dead in the eye and declares, "My wish is that wherever they've gone – they are both back on the ship by 23:00 hours!"

When the very curvaceous female midshipman at the Royal Naval Academy noticed that one of the men she was inspecting had an erection, she said to him, "And what do you call that trouser bulge, mister?"

The sailor looked her straight in the eye as he replied, "It's a one-gun salute, ma'am."

A young lieutenant had nearly completed his first overseas tour of sea duty when he was given an opportunity to display his ability at getting the ship under way. With an impressive array of well directed commands, he had the men busying about their tasks and, in no time, the ship had left port and was heading out of the channel.

The officer's efficiency was well noted by all aboard; some even claiming that he had set a new record for getting a destroyer under way. The young lieutenant was pleased as punch with his accomplishment, and was feeling pretty smug when a seaman approached him with a (no doubt congratulatory) message from the commander.

He was taken aback to discover that it was a radio message, and he was even more surprised when he read:

My personal congratulations upon completing your under-way preparation exercise efficiently, effectively and with amazing speed. Unfortunately, in your haste, you seem to have overlooked rule number one…

Be fucking sure that the Commander is aboard before getting the ship under way.

Q. What's black and blue and smells of seamen?

A. A Royal Navy uniform.

A marine walks in to the restroom and sees a sailor standing at the urinal, fussing with the thirteen buttons on his trousers.

The marine says, "It must be a pain in the arse to have to mess with all of those stupid buttons every time you take a piss."

The sailor replies, "Yes, it is! If I were a marine, all I'd have to do is take off my hat."

Somewhere in the Pacific a submariner received this letter from his girlfriend back home:

Dear Dan,

I can no longer continue our relationship. The distance between us is just too great. I must admit that I have cheated on you twice since you've been gone, and it's not fair to either of us. I'm sorry.

Could you please return the picture of me that I sent to you?

Love, Becky

The poor guy asked his crewmates for any snapshots they could spare of their girlfriends, sisters, ex-girlfriends, aunts, cousins etc. In addition to the picture of Becky, Dan included all the other pictures of the pretty girls he had collected from his mates. There were 57 photos in the envelope, along with this note:

Dear Becky,

I'm so sorry, but I can't quite remember which one you are. Please take your picture from the pile, and send the rest back to me.

Take care, Dan.

A young naval student was being put through the paces by an old sea captain.

"What would you do if a sudden storm sprang up on the starboard?"

"Throw out an anchor, sir," the student replied.

"What would you do if another storm sprang up aft?"

"Throw out another anchor, sir."

"And if another terrific storm sprang up forward, what would you do then?" asked the captain.

"Throw out another anchor, sir," came the reply.

"Hold on," said the captain. "Where are you getting all of those anchors from?"

"From the same place you're getting all of your storms, sir."

After being at sea in the Persian Gulf for 90 straight days, I said to the commanding officer, "Sir, I joined the navy to see the world, but for the past three months all I've seen is water."

"Lieutenant," the CO replied, "three-quarters of the earth is covered with water, and the navy has been showing you that. If you wanted to see the other quarter, you should have joined the Army."

BRITAIN'S NEW NAVY

The Royal Navy is proud of its new fleet of 'Type 45' destroyers. Having initially named the first two ships *HMS Audacious* and *HMS Resolute*, the Naming Committee has, after due consideration, renamed them *HMS Cautious* and *HMS Prudence*.

The next five ships are to be named:

HMS Empathy,
HMS Circumspect,
HMS Nervous,
HMS Timorous, and
HMS Apologist.

Costing £950 million each, they meet the needs of the 21st century and comply with the very latest employment, equality, health and safety and human rights law.

The new user-friendly crow's nest comes equipped with wheelchair access. Live ammunition has been replaced with paintballs to reduce the risk of anyone getting hurt and to cut down on the number of compensation claims. Stress counsellors and lawyers will be on duty 24 hours a day, and each ship will have its own on-board Industrial Tribunal.

The crew will be 50/50 men and women, and balanced in accordance with the latest Home Office directives on race, gender, sexuality and disability. Sailors will only have to work a maximum of 35 hours per week in line with EC regulations, even in wartime.

All vessels will come equipped with a maternity ward and nursery, situated on the same deck as the gay disco.

Tobacco will be banned throughout the ship, but cannabis will be allowed in the war-room and messes.

The Royal Navy is eager to shed its traditional reputation for '*Rum, sodomy and the lash*', so out goes the occasional rum ration, which is to be replaced by sparkling water.

Although sodomy remains, the lash will still be available, but only on request. Condoms can be obtained from the boatswain in a variety of flavours, except capstan full strength.

Saluting officers has been abolished because it is deemed elitist and is to be replaced by the more informal, "Hello, Sailor."

The Prime Minister said, "While these ships reflect the very latest in modern thinking, they are also capable of being upgraded to comply with any new legislation coming from Brussels."

His final words were, "Britannia waives the rules."

From the Diary of Julie Masterson, Second Lieutenant, *HMS Hornblower*, Royal Navy

July 1, 2011

Dear Diary:
Today began my first day on the seas with the Royal Navy. This really is a magnificent ship, although I do wonder how I am ever going to find my way around. I seem to be one of the only female ratings on board, but everyone has accepted me as part of the crew. The officers are friendly and I was personally summoned by the captain who was very interested in how I was settling in. He is the perfect example of a gentleman.

July 7
Dear Diary:
Today the captain asked me to dine with him at his very own table! How lucky I am to be invited to his stateroom. We talked and drank a glass of wine. Then he showed me his charts. He is some captain if he treats all newcomers to the ship to such an introduction.

July 14
Dear Diary:
Today, the captain summoned me again. He said that he had something urgent to ask me. I was thrilled that I was being singled out for a mission so soon. But he then made me an indecent proposal. I could not believe it! I denied his advances. I shudder to think that Naval decorum could come to this! What am I to do?

July 18
Dear Diary:
The captain again made advances to me today. I refused, as a good sailor should. He then gave me an ultimatum: either I sleep with him in three days, or he is going to do something drastic. I asked him what it was, he replied that he would sink the ship with everyone on board! Oh dear. What am I to do now?

July 21
Dear Diary:
Today I saved the lives of 2300 people.

A sailor in the Navy who had been at sea for a long time was anxious to be reunited with his girlfriend, so he sent her the following message a few days before his ship was due back in port:

I've missed you so much and I can't wait to make love to you. I want you to come down to the pier to meet me, and I want you to bring the van and have a mattress ready in the back so we can get down to it as soon as I step ashore.

The young lady, who was just as anxious to make love, sent him a reply:

I'll get the van ready, but you'd better be the first one off that ship, sailor, because I'm not checking ID cards.

The new rating aboard ship was beyond seasick. A warrant officer said, "Can I get you something?"

The young sailor replied, "How about an island?"

MISSING THE NAVY? TRY THESE SIMPLE STEPS TO HELP YOU FEEL AT HOME:

1. Send all friends and family away. Your only means of communication with them should be through letters that your neighbours have held for at least three weeks, after they have discarded two out of every five.

2. Invite people with disagreeable habits, bad body odour and sociability problems to come and live with you.

3. Unplug all radios and TVs to completely cut yourself off from the outside world. Once a month have a neighbour bring you a newspaper from six months before to keep you abreast of current events.

4. Monitor all home appliances and light switches, recording when everything is switched on and off.

5. Do not flush the toilet for five days to simulate the smell of 40 people using the same commode.

6. Lock the bathroom twice a day for a four-hour period.

7. Wear only military uniforms. Every four days, clean and press one dress uniform and wear it for 20 minutes.

8. Work in 19-hour cycles, sleeping only four hours at a time, to ensure that your body does not know or even care if it is day or night.

9. Cut a mattress in half and enclose three sides of your bed. Add a roof that prevents you from sitting up then place it on a platform that is four feet off the floor. Place a small dead animal under the bed to simulate the smell of your bunkmate's socks.

10. Set your alarm to go off at 10-minute intervals for the first hour of sleep and then randomly every two hours.

11. Have fruit and vegetables delivered to your garage and wait a week before eating them.

12. Periodically, shut off all power at the main circuit breaker and run around shouting "Fire! Fire! Fire!" and then restore power.

13. Routinely take a hoover, toaster or other appliance apart and put it back together.

14. Remove all plants, pictures and decorations. Paint everything grey. Repaint the interior of your home every month, whether it needs it or not.

15. Smash your forehead or shins with a hammer every two days to simulate collision injuries sustained on board.

16. Clean your house until there's not a speck of dust to be found. Call a stranger in to inspect it, telling them that they cannot leave until they find some fault, however trivial.

The three best things in life are a good landing, a good orgasm, and a good bowel movement... The night-carrier landing is one of the few opportunities in life where you get to experience all three at the same time.

HEAD IN
THE CLOUDS

NEVER FORGET...

1. Mankind has a perfect record in aviation; we never left one up there!

2. Every take-off is optional. Every landing is mandatory.

3. Flying isn't dangerous – crashing is what's dangerous.

4. Airspeed, altitude and brains. Two are always needed to successfully complete the flight.

5. Never fly in the same cockpit with someone braver than you.

6. It's always better to be down here wishing you were up there than up there wishing you were down here.

7. The ONLY time you have too much fuel is when you're on fire.

8. When in doubt, hold on to your altitude. No one has ever collided with the sky.

9. A 'good' landing is one from which you can walk away.
   A 'great' landing is one after which they can use the plane again.

10. You know you've landed with the wheels up if it takes full power to taxi to the ramp.

11. Always try to keep the number of landings you make equal to the number of take-offs you've made.

12. You start with a bag full of luck and an empty bag of experience. The trick is to fill the bag of experience before you empty the bag of luck.

13. In the on-going battle between objects made of aluminium going hundreds of miles per hour and the ground going zero miles per hour, the ground has yet to lose.

14. When one engine fails on a twin-engine airplane you always have enough power left to get you to the scene of the crash.

15. The three most useless things to a pilot are the altitude above you, the runway behind you, and a tenth of a second ago.

A station commander prided himself on his monthly "evening suppers" to which young junior officers were invited, with no option of refusal. Part of the evening ritual was to sample the commander's homemade wine. On this occasion, a thoroughly cheesed-off flying officer was called upon to attend for the umpteenth time.

The wine was duly served and all attendees tried not to show what they really thought of the 'plonk'. The flying officer had had enough. "Mmmm – unusual fragrance for such a young wine, sir. Where did you make it?" said he to the commander.

Delighted that someone had taken an interest, the senior officer replied, "In the kitchen, as a matter of fact."

"Oh really," responded the FO. "It doesn't travel very well, does it?"

A USAF F-16 is escorting an RAF Hercules when the F-16 pulls a perfect roll right round the Herc. The F-16 pilot then comes over the radio: "Let's see you try that, then."

The Hercules crew ponder for a moment, then shut down the number one engine.

A Herc crew member comes over the radio: "OK. Let's see you try that, then!"

The RAF are planning a flypast over Buckingham Palace. Due to budget restraints, they'll be on the easyJet flight from Luton to Barcelona.

Tower:	"Whisky Zulu 433, for noise abatement please turn right 45 degrees."
Whisky Zulu 433:	"Tower, we are at 35,000 feet. How much noise can we make up here?"
Tower:	"Sir, have you ever heard the noise an F-35 makes when it hits a Hercules?"

The teacher had given her Year Five class a project to ask their parents to tell them a story with a moral at the end of it.

"Sally, do you have a story to share?" the teacher asked.

"Yes, miss. My daddy told me a story about my Uncle Steve. He was a pilot in Afghanistan and his plane got hit. He had to bail out over enemy territory and all he had was a small flask of whisky, a pistol and a survival knife. He drank the whisky on the way down so that it wouldn't break and then his parachute landed right in the middle of twenty Taliban.

"He shot fifteen of them with his gun until he ran out of bullets, then he killed four more with his knife before the blade broke, and then he killed the last one with his bare hands."

"Good heavens," said the horrified teacher. "Did your daddy tell you the moral of this horrible story?"

"Yes, miss. Stay the fuck away from Uncle Steve when he's been drinking!"

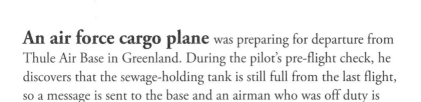

An air force cargo plane was preparing for departure from Thule Air Base in Greenland. During the pilot's pre-flight check, he discovers that the sewage-holding tank is still full from the last flight, so a message is sent to the base and an airman who was off duty is called out to take care of it.

The young man finally gets to the air base and makes his way to the aircraft, only to find that the pump truck has been left outdoors and is frozen solid – so he must find another one in the hangar, which takes even more time. He returns to the aircraft and is less than enthusiastic about what he has to do. Nevertheless, he goes about the pumping job deliberately and carefully.

As he's leaving the plane, the pilot stops him and says, "Son, your attitude and performance have caused this flight to be late and I'm going to personally see to it that you are not just reprimanded, but punished."

Shivering in the cold, the young airman takes a deep breath and says, "Sir, with all due respect, I'm not your son, I'm an airman in the RAF. I've been in Thule, Greenland, for 11 months without any leave, and reindeer arses are beginning to look pretty good to me. I have no stripes, it's two-thirty in the morning, the temperature is 40 degrees below zero, and my job here is to pump shit out of an aircraft. Now, sir, just exactly what form of punishment did you have in mind?"

Pointing to a pan of chicken wings and legs disguised in the classic mess-hall manner, a young airman asked the mess sergeant, "What's for scran?"

"Air Force Chicken," replied the sergeant. "You want wings or landing gear?"

A young airman was walking to the NAAFI for lunch, in uniform, minus his hat. A sergeant approached the crab and asked, "You, man! Where is your hat?"

"In my pocket," replied the airman.

"How come it's not on you head?" the sergeant demanded.

The airman answered, "Because I can't get my head in my pocket."

THE THREE MOST COMMON EXPRESSIONS IN AVIATION:

1. Why is it doing that?
2. Where are we?
3. Shit!

An RAF fighter pilot is flying over Afghanistan when he notices he is being flanked by two flying carpets piloted by men in flowing robes and armed with machine guns.

Responding to the threat, he manoeuvres and shoots them both out of the sky before returning to base.

When his commanding officer summons him he gets a right bollocking... Apparently they were Allied Carpets.

Q: What is the similarity between air traffic controllers and pilots?

A: If a pilot screws up, the pilot dies. If an ATC screws up… the pilot dies.

Q: How do you know when there is a fighter pilot in the building?

A: Don't worry, he'll come and tell you.

Q: "What made you take up skydiving?"

A: "A four-engine aircraft with three dead engines."

Q: If you don't know what rank an RAF officer is, what do you do?

A: Scan him with a barcode reader.

A trainee was on duty in the guardhouse when he heard a pounding on the door and the order, "Let me in!" Through the window he saw the uniform of the wing commander and immediately opened up. He quickly realized his mistake.

"Airman! Why didn't you check for my authority to enter?"

The airman replied, "Sir, you'd have gotten in anyway."

"What do you mean?"

"Uh… the hinges on the door… they're broken, sir."

"What? Show me!"

The airman opened the door, let the officer step out and slammed the door shut. The officer tried to open the door but it didn't budge.

"Airman! This door seems perfectly fine. Open up immediately!"

"Sorry, sir," said the airman, "may I see your authority to enter?"

A cocky young pilot liked to show off on the radio. Approaching an airfield at night he said, "Guess who?"

The tower controller switched the field lights off and replied, "Guess where!"

A navigator in a hot air balloon realized he was lost. He lowered altitude and spotted a man on the ground below. He shouted to him, "Excuse me, can you help me? I promised a friend that I would meet him an hour ago, but I don't know where I am."

The man consulted his portable GPS and replied, "You're in a hot air balloon approximately 30 feet above a ground elevation of 2,346 feet above sea level. You are 51 degrees, 53.97 minutes north latitude and 3 degrees, 49.09 minutes west longitude."

The balloonist rolled his eyes and said, "You must be an engineer."

"I am," replied the man. "How did you know?"

"Well," answered the balloonist, "everything you told me is technically correct, but I have no idea what to make of your information, and I'm still lost. Frankly, you've not been much help to me at all."

The man smiled and responded, "You must be an RAF officer."

"I am," replied the balloonist. "But how did you know?"

"Well," said the man, "you don't know where you are or where you're going. You've risen to where you are due to a large quantity of hot air. You've made a promise that you have no idea how to keep, and now you expect *me* to solve your problem. You're in exactly the same position you were in before we met, but somehow, now, it's *my* fault."

Q: How do you know that you are talking to an RAF pilot?

A: After two hours he will say, "Anyway, that's enough about me, tell me about yourself."

Q: What is the difference between RAF aircrew and God?

A: God does not think he is aircrew!

Q: Why are RAF cooks called Fitters and Turners?

A: Because they fit food into pots and turn it into...

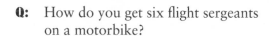

Q: How do you get six flight sergeants on a motorbike?

A: Promote one to warrant officer, the others will soon crawl up his arse!

Q: What's the difference between a jet engine and a pilot?

A: After the sortie, the jet stops whining.

Q: How many pilots does it take to change a light bulb?

A: Just one to hold it still while the rest of the world revolves around him.

WORST RAF PILOT CHAT-UP LINES:

"When I look at you, my pants fly in formation."

"I left my fighter jet in the hangar – I badly need my sump draining."

"They call me Hercules: Takes a while to get me up, but, when I'm up, I'm up for hours."

"You've just been targeted by a heat-seeking missile of love."

"My landing gear's up – just give me a signal and I'll approach."

"I can still fly four missions a night, if you know what I mean."

"I'm looking for a place to land my stealth bomber."

"You've got me flying by the seat of your pants."

A BBC TV journalist is interviewing a elderly former Polish fighter pilot.

Interviewer: "Mr Jankowski, I understand that in 1943 you shot down five German aircraft in a single engagement. Could you tell us what happened?"

Polish fighter pilot:

"Well, we were flying at 20,000 feet when we spotted five Fokkers flying along below us. So we dived down and I aimed at one of the Fokkers, fired a burst from my machine guns right into him and he exploded. Then I saw that one of the Fokkers was on my tail, so I pulled round in a loop and got behind him, fired, and he went down on fire. I looked around and saw two Fokkers attacking my squadron leader, so slipped in behind them, fired, and that was another Fokker going down in flames. The other Fokker tried to get away from me, but I got right up behind him, blasted him with my machine guns, and he turned over and exploded. There was only one of the Fokkers left now, and he was trying to get away, but I flew up behind him, shot – bang, bang, bang – and he blew up too!"

Interviewer:

"I should point out for the benefit of the viewers at home, that the Fokker was a type of German aircraft used in the war."

Polish fighter pilot:

"No, no, no – these fokkers were Messerschmitts!"

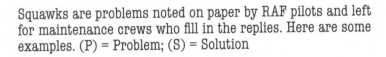

Squawks are problems noted on paper by RAF pilots and left for maintenance crews who fill in the replies. Here are some examples. (P) = Problem; (S) = Solution

1. (P) Left inside tyre almost needs replacement.
   (S) Almost replaced left inside tyre.

2. (P) Test flight OK, except autoland very rough.
   (S) Autoland not installed on this aircraft.

3. (P) No. 2 propeller seeping hydraulic fluid.
   (S) No. 2 propeller seepage normal. Nos. 1, 3 and 4 lack normal seepage.

4. (P) Something loose in cockpit.
   (S) Something tightened in cockpit.

5. (P) Evidence of hydraulic-fluid leak on main right landing gear.
   (S) Removed evidence of hydraulic-fluid leak on main right landing gear.

6. (P) DME volume unbelievably loud.
   (S) DME volume set to a more believable level.

7. (P) Dead insects on windshield.
   (S) Live insects on order.

8. (P) Autopilot in altitude hold mode produces a 200-feet-per-minute descent.
   (S) Unable to reproduce problem on ground.

9. (P) IFF inoperative.
   (S) IFF always inoperative when set to OFF mode.

10. (P) Friction lock causes throttle levers to stick.
    (S) That is what they are supposed to do.

11. (P) No. 3 engine missing.
    (S) No. 3 engine found after brief search of right wing.

12. (P) Aircraft handles funny.
    (S) Aircraft told to be serious.

13. (P) Target radar hums.
    (S) Target radar reprogrammed with the right words.

My brother is an RAF pilot. Just last week he accepted a posting in Seoul. "What on Earth made you do that?" I said. "You had a cushy number at home!"
"Well," he replied. "It sounded like a good Korea move."

Newton's Law states that what goes up, must come down. Our Wing Commander's Law states that *what goes up and comes down had damn well better be able to go back up again*!

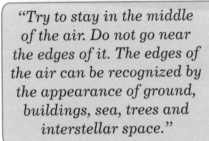

"Try to stay in the middle of the air. Do not go near the edges of it. The edges of the air can be recognized by the appearance of ground, buildings, sea, trees and interstellar space."

"A pilot is a confused soul who talks about women when he's flying, and about flying when he's with a woman."

Air Force One was flying over the UK and called up a USAF base "Requesting Radar".

"What is your position?" asked Air Traffic Control.

"You got radar, you find us," Air Force One replied.

After a few minutes, ATC announced, "Air Force One, we're changing frequency."

"What frequency are you changing to?" asked Air Force One.

"You've got 720 channels – you find us!" ATC replied.

God might be my co-pilot, but the Devil is my bombardier.

A trainee pilot became lost during his first solo flight. While attempting to locate the aircraft on radar, air traffic control asked, "What is your last known position and we'll try to locate you."

The trainee pilot replied, "Well, I was number one for take-off."

FOREIGN

LEGIONS

The French Government announced today that it is imposing a ban on the use of fireworks at Disneyland Paris. The decision comes the day after a nightly fireworks display at the park – located just 30 miles outside Paris – caused soldiers at a nearby French Army garrison to surrender to a group of Czech tourists.

A tourist visiting a small town in Israel came upon a statue dedicated to 'The Unknown Soldier'. At the base of the statue, a plaque declared: 'Here lies Jakob Goldberg'.

The tourist enquired of one of the locals how was it possible that an unknown had a name. The resident replied, "As a soldier, that Jakob was pretty much unknown, but as an accountant – Oy! He was really something."

The French Government has recently raised its terror alert level from 'Run' to 'Hide'.

The only two higher levels in France are 'Surrender' and 'Collaborate'. The rise was precipitated by a recent fire that destroyed France's white flag factory, effectively paralysing the country's military capability.

The Germans also increased their alert state from 'Disdainful Arrogance' to 'Dress in Uniform and Sing Marching Songs.' They also have two higher levels: 'Invade a Neighbour' and 'Lose'.

Italy has increased the alert level from 'Shout loudly and excitedly' to 'Elaborate Military Posturing'. Two more levels remain: 'Ineffective Combat Operations', and 'Change Sides'.

Back in the 70s, a man was wandering the streets of Belfast late one night. All of a sudden a man wearing a balaclava jumped out in front of him, thrust a sawn-off shotgun in his face and demanded "What the feck are ye? A Catholic or Protestant?"

The man smiled and responded, "Actually, I'm Jewish."

The masked gunman chuckled, "Well, I must be the luckiest Arab in Ulster tonight!"

An IRA active service unit is waiting in the undergrowth in the wilds of south Armagh for a British Army patrol to pass by.

"What time is it?" says one.

"Half past four," says the other.

"That's funny. The patrol was due here at four o'clock," says the first. "I hope nothing's happened to them."

An American admiral was attending a conference that included admirals from both the Royal Navy and the French Navy. At a cocktail reception, he found himself in a small group that included personnel from both navies.

The French admiral started complaining that Europeans had to learn many languages but Americans spoke only English. He asked, "Why is it that we have to speak English in these conferences rather than you speaking French?"

Without hesitating, the American admiral replied, "Maybe it is because the Brits, Canadians, Aussies and Americans arranged it so that you would not have to speak German."

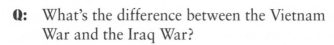

Q: What's the difference between the Vietnam War and the Iraq War?

A: George W. Bush had a plan to get out of the Vietnam War.

Q: What is the first thing that the French Army teaches in basic training?

A: How to surrender in at least ten languages.

Q: Where did Napoleon keep his armies?

A: Up his sleevies.

Q: What do you get when a grenade is thrown into a French kitchen?

A: Linoleum Blownapart.

Q: What's the most useful item in a French tank?

A: The rear-view mirror.

The two servicemen were escaping from the POW camp by scaling the fence. One stumbled and the guard called, "Halt! Who goes there?"

"Meow!" came the reply from the first, and away he crept into the night.

The second stumbled and the guard again called, "Halt! Who goes there?"

He answered, "Another cat!"

The easiest kind of 'ship' to wreck is a relationship. Hang on, I'm sorry, scrap that. I was forgetting about the French Navy.

A French girl came home, sobbing because she was pregnant.

"Who is the father of the child?" her father demanded.

"Well, he is the most famous man in France," she sobbed.

"What? The President?!" said her father incredulously.

Through her tears she spluttered, "No, papa, the Unknown Soldier!"

Back in the days of the Troubles, an Irish travelling salesman was stopped at a British Army checkpoint in Armagh. The soldier said, "Get out of the car and open the boot!"

The salesman responded by pleading, "I'm sorry, but the handbrake on the car is broken. I can't take my foot off the brake or it'll roll back down the hill."

The soldier replied, "Are you taking the piss?" Then he slid into the passenger seat, and stamps his big boot on to the brake pedal. "Now go and open the boot!"

The salesman reluctantly complied with the soldier's request, and went and opened the boot of the car. "Now tell me," shouted the soldier from inside the car, "are there any weapons in there?"

A career US military man, who had retired as a corporal, was telling the younger men how he handled officers during his years of service.

"It didn't matter a hoot if he was a lieutenant, a colonel or the commander-in-chief. I always told those guys exactly where to get off."

"Wow, you must have been something," the admiring young soldiers remarked. "What was your job in the service?"

"Elevator operator in the Pentagon," he replied.

Have you heard about the worst-ever firing squad? They all stood in a circle!

The Presidents of Russia and the United States are walking along the beach. They start discussing their submarines. The Russian President says,

"We recently have made much progress with our submarines. They can now stay submerged as long as yours, for one month."

The US President smiles, "We've been developing our subs too. They can can now stay underwater for two months." Suddenly they hear a strange sound coming from the sea. An old-fashioned submarine appears. A hatch opens and a uniformed man appears.

"Heil Hitler, meine Herren! Can you tell me whether the war is over yet?"

In 1999, France's elite paratroopers changed their name in order to 'reflect their new role in helping to defend the entire European Union'. Well, that's what their spokesman claimed.

Possibly the real reason was that they were now working with groups that speak English. Their old name '*Commandos de Recherche et d'Action en Profondeur*' (Long-Range Search and Action Commandos) had become too embarrassing. Those proud French soldiers really didn't want to admit that their organization was CRAP!

A company in the Foreign Legion had spent three years in the Sahara desert, never having seen a woman. They finally decide to send one lucky private to the nearest town to spend some time with a woman and tell them all about it.

A few days later the private comes back all happy and relaxed. The whole company crowds around him waiting to hear of his great escapades.

"On the third day…" he begins.

"No! No! start with the first day," everyone shouts in chorus.

"On the third day," the private continues, "she asked me to stop so she could go to the bathroom…"

A reporter is driving a jeep in the desert. She sees a captain in the French Foreign Legion pulling and tugging on a camel, but the camel won't budge. She stops and says, "Captain, do you need some help with the camel?"

The legionnaire tells her that the camel won't budge but she's welcome to try. The reporter gets out of the jeep, takes two bricks from the back and *pow!…* smashes the camel's testicles with the bricks. The camel makes a terrible noise and runs off into the desert. The captain drops his pants and says, "Great! Now do the same to me. I've got to take that son of a bitch back to camp!"

The USAF chief of staff decided that he would personally intervene in the recruiting crisis affecting all of the armed services. He directed a nearby air force base to open and instructed that all eligible young men and women from the neighbourhood should be invited to look around.

As he and his staff were standing near a brand-new F-22 fighter, a pair of twin brothers who looked like they had just stepped out of a Marine Corps recruiting poster walked up to them. The chief of staff stuck out his hand and introduced himself. He looked at the first young man and asked,

"Son, what skills can you bring to the air force?"

The young man looked at him and said, "Pilot!"

The General became excited, turned to his aide and said, "Get him in today, all the paperwork done, everything, do it!"

The aide hustled the young man off. The general looked at the second young man and asked, "What skills do you bring to the air force?"

The young man said, "I chop wood!"

"Son," the general replied, "we don't need wood choppers in the United States Air Force. What do you know how to do?"

"I chop wood!"

"Young man," huffed the general, "you are not listening to me, we don't need wood choppers, this is the twenty-first century!"

"Well," the young man said, "you hired my brother!"

"Of course we did," said the general, "he's a pilot!"

The young man rolled his eyes and said, "So what? I have to chop it before he can pile it!"

The French Foreign Legion have been lost in the desert for nine days with no water supplies when they come to the brow of a sand dune and look down into the valley and see a small town. Expecting it to be a mirage, the captain, second officer and the rest of the men trudge wearily down the side of the hill. To their delight, however, the town is real and a small caravan of nomadic tribesmen have set up a market.

The legionnaires enter the market, hoping to quench their thirst. They go to the first stall where the captain says to the stallholder, "We are the French Foreign Legion and we have been lost in the desert for nine days. We must have water and will pay any price."

The nomad simply shrugs his shoulders and says, "I have no water. I have only sponge cake."

Disappointed, the legionnaires move to the next stall and the captain again demands, "We are the French Foreign Legion and we have been lost in the desert for nine days. We must have water and will pay any price." The second stallholder simply shrugs and says, "Alas, I have no water. All I have is cold custard."

The legionnaires decide to try the third stall and, once again, the captain accosts the nomadic tribesman minding the stall and demands, "We are the French Foreign Legion and we have been lost in the desert for nine days. We must have water and will pay any price."

The third stallholder shakes his head slowly with a frown on his face and replies, "I have no water to sell. All I have is strawberry jelly."

Despairing, the legionnaires try the final stall. Again, the captain demands water from the stallholder and again the tribesman cannot oblige. "Alas, my stall has only whipped cream for sale. That, and little multi-coloured sprinkles. I have no water."

The legionnaires give up hope at this point and decide to set off in search of water at an oasis or another town. As they walk back up the hill, out of the valley and away from the market, the captain turns to his second officer and asks, "Is it just me, or did you find that all a little odd?"

To which the second officer replies, "It was a trifle bazaar, sir!"

War is just God's way of teaching Americans geography.

FRIENDLY
FIRE

REGIMENTAL NICKNAMES

There is a long, and sometimes noble, tradition of regimental nicknames in the British armed forces – some going back to the Napoleonic era. Regiments have often given themselves highfalutin' names such as the 9th/12th Royal Lancers, who like to think their nickname is the Delhi Spearmen after their actions in the Indian Mutiny in 1857.

However, the modern forces, being what they are, seem to prefer to find their own imaginative names for their rivals – the 9th/12th RL are more likely to be referred to as the Three Quarter Prancers or the Ballroom Dancers.

Still, looking at the list below, it could be worse...

The Agile and Suffering Highlanders	The Argyll and Sutherland Highlanders
Andy Capp's Commandos	Army Catering Corps
The Armoured Farmers	The Devon and Dorset Light Infantry
Ballroom Dancers	9th/12th Royal Lancers
Bedpan Mechanics	RAF Medical Branch
The Bing Crosbies	The King's Own Scottish Borderers
Blanket Stackers or Provisional Wing of Tescos .	Royal Logistics Corps
The Boneheads	The Queen's Royal Lancers
The Broken Biscuits	The Royal Scots
Cabbageheads	Royal Marine Commandos
The Cavalry	The Royal Tank Regiment
Cherry Berries or Birdshit	The Parachute Regiment
Di's Guys (or Camilla's Gorillas or The Squidgies)	The Princess of Wales' Royal Regiment
Donkey Wallopers or Piccadilly Cowboys	The Royal Household Cavalry
The Drop Shorts, Nine-Mile Snipers or The Royal Arselickers	Royal Artillery

The Foreskins	Royal Inniskilling Fusiliers and 5th Royal Inniskilling Dragoon Guards
The Frankies	The Green Howards
The Green Slime	Intelligence Corps
Have Another Cocktail	HAC (The Honourable Artillery Company)
Hell's Latest Invention	Highland Light Infantry
The Ladies from Hell	Black Watch
The M4 Rifles	Royal Gloucestershire, Berkshire and Wiltshire Regiment
Pontius Pilate's Bodyguard	Royal Scots
Queen's Dancing Girls	1st Queen's Dragoon Guards
Run Away Someone's Coming	RASC (Royal Army Service Corps)
Scaleybacks	Royal Signals
The Shite Hawks	The King's Royal Hussars
The Slashers	28th Regiment of Foot
Snot Hats	The Royal Intelligence Corps
Snowdrops	RAF Military Police
Special Pen Service	SPS (Staff and Personnel Support)
Teeny-weeny Airways	The Army Air Corps
The Tots	17th Lancers
The Vein Openers	29th Regiment of Foot
The Vulgar Fraction	16th/5th The Queen's Royal Lancers
Wedgeheads	The Royal Engineers
Wooden Tops	Brigade of Guards
Woofers	Worcestershire and Sherwood Foresters

ROYAL MARINES RULES:

1. Be courteous to everyone, friendly to no one.

2. When necessary, be aggressive enough, quickly enough.

3. Have a plan.

4. Have a back-up plan, because the first one probably won't work.

5. Be polite. Be professional. But, have a plan to kill everyone you meet, even your friends.

6. Do not attend a gunfight with a handgun whose calibre does not start with a '4'.

7. Anything worth shooting is worth shooting twice. Ammo is cheap. Life is expensive.

8. Move away from your attacker. Distance is your friend.

9. Use cover or concealment as much as possible.

10. Flank your adversary when possible. Protect your own.

11. Always cheat, always win. The only unfair fight is the one you lose.

12. If you are not shooting, you should be communicating your intention to shoot.

ARMY RULES:

1. Curse bitterly when receiving an operational order.

2. Make sure there is extra ammo and extra coffee.

3. Curse bitterly.

4. Curse bitterly.

5. Do not listen to second lieutenants; it can get you killed.

6. Curse bitterly.

SAS RULES:

1. Walk 50 miles wearing a 75-pound rucksack having eaten virtually nothing for 24 hours.

2. Locate individuals that require killing.

3. Request permission via radio from 'Command' to perform killing.

4. Curse bitterly when mission is aborted.

SBS RULES:

1. Look very cool in sunglasses.

2. Fire at anything and everything within view.

3. Adjust Speedos.

4. Check hair in mirror.

RAF RULES:

1. Have a cocktail.

2. Adjust temperature on air-conditioner.

3. See what's on Sky Sports.

4. Request more funding from Government with a 'killer' PowerPoint presentation.

6. Host gala evening for MPs, MOD and Defence industry executives.

7. Receive funding, set up new command and assemble assets.

8. Declare the assets 'strategic' but never deploy them operationally.

9. Make sure that the base is as far as possible from the conflict but close enough to have tax exemption.

ROYAL NAVY RULES:

1. Go to sea.

2. Drink rum.

3. Deploy marines.

It has long been said that the Royal Navy has traditions, the Army has customs and the RAF has dirty habits.

WHEN THE SHIT HITS THE FAN...

The seaman who has been at sea for six months fires off a missile and declares,
"This is the shit!"

The squaddie who is parachuted into a combat zone under a hail of enemy fire with explosions going off all around shouts,
"Wooo! I was born for this shit!"

The airman who gets into his rental car, drives, checks into his five-star hotel, walks into his room and discovers that the internet connection is down and growls,
"For Christ's sake, what kind of shit is this?"

One day, a wing commander, an admiral and a general were hiking together and unexpectedly came upon a wide, raging and violent river. They needed to get to the other side, but had no idea of how to do so.

The wing commander called out to God, praying, "Please, God, give me the strength to cross this river."

PFFFT!

God gave him big arms and strong legs, and he was able to swim across. However, it took him more than an hour, and he almost drowned a couple of times.

Seeing this, the admiral prayed to God, saying, "Please, God, give me the strength and tools to cross this river."

PFFFT!

God gave him a rowboat and oars. He was able to row across but it still took almost an hour, as it was very rough, and he almost capsized several times.

The army general saw how things worked out for the other two, so when he prayed to God, he said, "Please, God, give me the strength, tools and the intelligence to cross this river."

PFFFT!

God turned him into a lance corporal. He looked at the map, hiked upstream a couple of hundred yards, and walked across the bridge.

A little boy was standing in front of a mirror in the toilets at Heathrow Airport, when in walked a Royal Marines staff sergeant in his dress blues. The little boy turned to the marine and asked,

"Wow! Are you a Royal Marine?"

The marine replied, "Why yes, I am, young man. Would you like to wear my hat?"

"Oh, could I?" asked the little boy. He took the hat and placed it on his head and turned to admire himself in the mirror. As he was looking in the mirror, he heard the door open and a paratrooper entered the room. The little boy turned and went over to the soldier and said, "Excuse me, sir. Are you a paratrooper?"

The para replied in a thunderous voice, "Why yes, I am! Would you like to shine my boots?"

The little boy smiled, and said, "Oh, no, sir! I'm not really a marine; I'm just wearing his hat!"

Two junior officers on a course at a joint services staff college went to the toilet to use the urinals prior to going to lunch. The Army officer finished first and went to the wash basin and washed his hands. As he was drying them the RAF officer finished and headed for the door. His companion said, "At Sandhurst they teach us to wash our hands after using the toilet."

Back came the reply, "Is that so? At Cranwell they teach us not to piss on our hands."

A soldier, a sailor, an airman and a Royal Marine get into an argument about which force is the best. The argument gets so heated that they fail to see an oncoming truck. They are all hit and killed instantly. When they arrive in Heaven, they see Saint Peter at the Pearly Gates and decide that he can settle their argument. They ask him, "Saint Peter, what military service is the best?" He thinks for a moment, and then says, "Well, I'm afraid I can't tell you, but I'll tell you what. I'll talk to God next time I see Him, and I'll find out for you. In the meantime, welcome to Heaven." So they enter.

Later, while walking around, they see Saint Peter and remind him about their question. Before Saint Peter can say anything, trumpets sound, a bright light shines, and a white dove flies out of the light with an envelope in its beak. Saint Peter says, "Ah, here's the answer from the Boss." He takes the letter, and the dove flies off. He opens it, trumpets play, gold dust flies up, and Saint Peter reads aloud:

FROM: THE DESK OF GOD
TO: SOLDIERS, SAILORS, AIRMEN AND ROYAL MARINES
RE: WHICH SERVICE IS BEST.

Dear Soldiers, Sailors, Airmen and Marines,

All branches of the British Military are equally honourable. You should take great pride in serving in Her Majesty's Armed Forces in any capacity.
Therefore, there is no superior service.

Sincerely,
God, C-IN-C FLEET (Ret.)

While serving in Belize, a young private supplemented his personal items of toiletries by writing to various manufacturers of said products, praising their durability and usefulness in the hot, humid climate of the jungle. Invariably, he would receive a reply and a small parcel containing samples of the product, which he used or sold to his mates.

A junior RAF officer heard of this wheeze and decided to try it. He wrote to Gillette, telling them that he'd been using the same blade, in the jungle, for a year and it was as good as the day he bought it. Gillette replied, thanking him and saying that they had great pleasure in enclosing another year's supply!

An air base had military aircraft based on one side and civilian aircraft on the other, with the control tower in the middle. One day the tower received a call from an aircraft asking,

"What time is it?"

The tower responded, "Who is calling?"

The aircraft replied, "What difference does it make?"

The tower replied, "It makes a lot of difference. If you're a civilian flight, it's 3 o'clock. If you're Royal Air Force, it is 15:00 hours. If you're a Royal Navy aircraft, it is 6 bells. If you're an army aircraft, the big hand is on the 12 and the little hand is on the 3. And, if you're a Royal Marines aircraft, it's Thursday afternoon."

Q: Why wasn't the RAF involved in the Battle of Waterloo?

A: It was fought on a Sunday.

Q: What's the difference between a marine and a piece of toast?

A: You can make a soldier out of a piece of toast.

Q: What's the difference between a Royal Marine and an endowment policy?

A: An endowment policy usually matures after 25 years!

At a bar an RAF pilot leans over to the well-muscled man beside him and says, "Do you want to hear a joke about the stupid paras?"

The man replies, "Before you tell the joke, you should know something. I'm in 2 Para. The guy sitting next to me is six-foot-two feet 2, weighs 225 pounds, and he's also a para. The barman is six-foot-five, 250 pounds and he's an ex-para. Now, are you sure you want to tell that joke?"

The pilot raises an eyebrow, turns away and says, "No, forget it. I can't be bothered to explain it three times."

113

One day, four recruiters were sitting in their joint service office, moaning about the lack of qualified applicants. They were short of their monthly goal, but the only prospective recruits had scored far too low on their aptitude tests.

All four looked up as an old man in a white lab coat entered, carrying a small metal box. "He can't want to enlist," they all thought. "He's far too old."

The elderly scientist said, "I've heard about your recruiting problems, and I have the answer! I have discovered that the perfect military recruit has an IQ of between 110.8 and 135.7. The exact IQ determines exactly which military job a person is best suited for. This machine which can actually increase a person's IQ to match a specified IQ within this range."

"If this works, it's fantastic," the four recruiters thought. They quickly got on the phone and called some of the unqualified recruits, and asked them to come down to the office to try a new method of qualifying.

The first unqualified recruit to show up wanted to be a marine. The Royal Marines recruiter told the scientist, "I'd like him to be qualified for infantry." The scientist replied, "OK, let's see, that's an ideal IQ of 111.2." The scientist made an adjustment to the machine and hooked it up to the recruit's temples. The starting meter showed an IQ of 87. The scientist pushed a red button on top of the machine, and PFFF! The needle shot up to 111.2. They all watched in anticipation as the recruit retook the qualification test. The results were perfect for infantry!

"I'd like the next recruit to be qualified for the Parachute Regiment," said the army recruiter.

The scientist set his machine at 115.3. The beginning needle showed 65, but as soon as the scientist pressed the red button, it jumped up to 115.3. The resultant test results showed him to be perfect for 2 Para.

"I'd like the next one to be qualified for submarines," said the navy recruiter. The scientist set his machine at 117.6. The beginning needle showed 69, but as soon as the scientist pressed the red button, it jumped up to 117.6. The resultant test showed him to be perfect for submarine duty.

Finally, the air force recruit showed up. When the scientist hooked up the machine, he frowned. The recruit's IQ showed 190. The scientist said, "This recruit's problem is that he's too intelligent for the service. In order to make him fit in, I'll have to decrease his IQ, and I've never tried that before."

"Please try it," urged the RAF recruiter, who did not want to explain how the army, navy, and royal marines had been able to recruit someone this day, and he had not.

"We'll make him a group captain," said the scientist. "I'll set the machine to lower his IQ to 125.1." But when the scientist hit the button, the needle immediately travelled down to 25!

The scientist ripped the hook-ups off the recruit's head, and screamed, "Oh, my God! How do you feel?"

The recruit replied, "I feel fine! My flaps are up, gear is down, and I'm ready for take-off!"

The SAS, the infantry and the military police decide to go on a survival weekend together to see who comes out top. After some basic exercises, the trainer tells them that their next objective is to go down into the woods and come back with a rabbit for tea.

First up are the SAS. They don their infra-red goggles, drop to the ground and crawl into the woods in formation. Absolute silence follows for five minutes, followed by a loud bang and a single muffled shot. They emerge with a rabbit, shot cleanly through the forehead.

"Excellent," says the trainer.

Next up are the infantry. They finish their cans of lager, cover themselves in camouflage cream, fix bayonets and charge down into the woods, screaming at the top of their lungs. For the next hour the woods ring with the sound of machine-gun fire, mortar bombs, hand grenades and bloodcurdling war cries. Eventually, they emerge, carrying the charred remains of a rabbit.

"A bit messy, but you got a result. Well done," says the trainer.

Finally, in go the MPs, walking slowly, hands behind backs, looking up in the trees. For the next few hours, the silence is only broken by the occasional crackle of a radio: "Sierra Oscar One, suspect headed straight for you," etc. After what seems like an eternity, they emerge, escorting a squirrel in handcuffs.

"What the hell do you think you're doing?" asks the incredulous trainer. "Take this squirrel back and get me a rabbit, like I asked you five hours ago!"

So back they go. Minutes pass. Minutes turn to hours, day turns to night. The next morning the trainer and the rest of the crew are awakened by the MPs holding the squirrel which is now covered in bruises.

"Are you taking the piss?" asks the seriously irate trainer.

The military police team leader shoots a glance at the squirrel, who squeaks: "All right, all right, I'll talk. I confess... I'm a fucking rabbit."

The Queen is inspecting three armed forces personnel, one from each of her fighting forces. She asks each one what they would do if they woke up and found a rat in their tent while on operations.

The squaddie says, "I'd reach over, grab my bayonet and stab it to death!"

The matelot says, "I'd reach over, grab my boot and batter it to death!"

The airman says, "I'd reach over, pick up my phone, call reception and ask 'Who the fuck has put a tent up in my hotel room?'"

DIFFERENCES BETWEEN INFANTRY, ARMOURED CORPS AND ARTILLERY

HAPPINESS IS...

Infantry: A good rifle.

Armoured: A big tank.

Artillery: Any loud boom.

UPON HEARING FIREWORKS...

Infantry: Cool, just like a live fire exercise.

Armoured: Not loud enough.

Artillery: Fireworks? What fireworks?

OTHER SERVICES...

Infantry: Waste of rations.

Armoured: Waste of rations.

Artillery: Waste of rations.

BIGGEST LUXURY IN THE FIELD...

Infantry: Engineers blowing trenches for them.

Armoured: Grunts to dig their trenches for them.

Artillery: Cable TV.

A LONG ROUTE MARCH WITH FULL KIT...

Infantry: 20k.

Armoured: From the hangars to the tank.

Artillery: What's a route march?

OFFICERS...

Infantry: ... are morons and should stay away from the trench lines.

Armoured: ... are morons and should stay out of the vehicles.

Artillery: ... are morons and should stay away from the gun lines.

FAVOURITE MODE OF TRANSPORTATION...

Infantry: Anything but walking.

Armoured: Tanks. Tanks. Tanks.

Artillery: Don't you have to move around to require transport?

BIGGEST GRIPE IN THE FIELD...

Infantry: The weather.

Armoured: Coffee maker in tank not working.

Artillery: Only having basic cable TV package.

BREAKFAST IN THE FIELD...

Infantry: I don't care what it is, just as long as I can sit down to eat it.

Armoured: Hot coffee and whisky with a beer chaser.

Artillery: Fried eggs, crispy bacon, sausages, toast and fresh coffee.

BACK IN THE DAY

Back in the days of National Service, a young recruit was determined to fail his physical. When the doctor ordered him to read the eye chart, he answered, "What eye chart?"

"The one on the wall, smartarse!" bellowed the doctor.

"What wall?" bluffed the man, determined not to be beaten so easily.

With that, the doctor marched out to reception and spoke to his attractive young receptionist.

Minutes later she walked into the surgery – stark naked. A gorgeous sight, she stood right in front of the chart.

"Now what do you see?" chuckled the doctor.

But the recruit was desperate to make his ruse pay off. "I can't see a thing, sir. I'm afraid I must be as blind as a bat."

The doctor handed him a chit, saying, "Well, you may not see anything, but your dick is pointing straight to Catterick! Welcome to the army!"

Two men were boasting to each other about their old army days. "Why, my outfit was so well-drilled," declared one, "that when they presented arms all you could hear was slap, slap, click."

"Very good," conceded the other. "But when my company presented arms you'd just hear slap, slap, jingle."

"What was the jingle?" asked the first.

"Oh," replied the other in an off-hand manner. "Just our medals."

One smart-arse was convinced he could escape conscription by outwitting the doc at his physical. During his examination, the doctor asked him, "Now, can you read the letters on the wall?"

"What letters?" he answered.

"Good," said the doctor. "You passed the hearing test."

A group of friends meet in a pub after one of them has returned from his National Service medical. He recounts that, towards the end of the examination, the doctor asked him to drop his trousers and enquired how long he had been wearing a truss.

The boy says he told the doctor, "About six years", and the doctor then wrote 'MU' in large red letters on the youth's file. The boy asked the doctor what this meant, and the doctor explained that 'MU' stands for 'Medically Unfit' because he had been wearing a truss for so long.

Another youth, who due to have his medical in a few days, asks his friend if he can borrow a truss in order to be declared unfit for military service. The same process is followed. When the second youth drops his trousers, the medic asks how long the boy has been wearing a truss. "About five or six years," comes the reply, at which point the doctor writes 'ME' on the candidate's file in large blue letters.

"Excuse me, but shouldn't that be 'MU' for medically unfit because I wear a truss?" asks the boy.

"No," replies the doctor. "'ME' stands for Middle East. If you can wear a truss back-to-front for six years, you're fit enough to ride a camel."

The Korean War was at the height of the fighting. In one British company the captain was having his doubts about the sanity of one of his charges and didn't want to trust him with a real weapon.

Instead of a gat, the young soldier was issued with a broom. The sergeant told him that if he pointed the broom at the target and yelled "Bang-bang!" it would be just as effective.

He did as ordered – as the rest of the company fired away they could hear him shouting, "Bang, Bang, Bang-bang." The private seemed happy enough, joining in the after-battle boasts about how many Koreans he had laid to waste. Then, amazingly, the other men began to notice he really was felling the enemy. Somehow, it was working and he became their lucky magic mascot.

They had come through every fire-fight successfully, as his broom put paid to attack after attack. Then, after four months of patrolling, ambushes and forays, his unit finally got involved in a major skirmish. As all hell broke loose, their trusted 'Guardian of the Broom' raised his weapon and, yelling "Bang-bang" or "Brat-a tat-tat" (for he had now gone automatic), he wasted every enemy soldier that assaulted their position... except one! No matter what he did, this lone Korean kept coming at him.

"Bang-bang, Brat-a-tat-tat." Over and over they heard him try to stop the enemy soldier in his tracks. Then all of a sudden through the dust and smoke of the attack, they saw the young soldier laying there seriously wounded. As they tended their hero they followed his pointing finger and watched in dismay as his assailant continued across the battlefield, his arm pointed out in front, yelling, "Clank! Clank! I'm a tank! Clank! Clank! I'm a tank!"

The Roman galley was approaching its home port after a successful deployment. The captain could see the crowds on the jetty waiting to welcome the ship home and he decided to show off and ordered "Maximum speed!" The beat of the timing drum gradually increased tempo as the oars picked up speed.

Suddenly there was the sound of oars striking each other and the ship slewed to starboard and came to a stop. The slave-master went through the rowing decks until he came to a slave slumped dead over his oar. Two deck hands came below, unchained the dead slave, carried the body up on deck and threw it over the side.

The slave-master then went through the rowing decks again, lashing every slave across the back. When he returned to his position at the timing drum he shouted, "You know what to do!"

As one, all the galley slaves leant back and urinated into the air. Once the ship was under way again one of the slaves asked the man he shared an oar with, "What was that all about?"

"Oh, it's a tradition in the Roman Navy, every time someone leaves the ship, we have a whip round and a piss-up."

The knight returned to the king's castle with prisoners, bags of gold and other riches from his victories.

"Tell me of your battles," said the king.

"Well, sire, I have been robbing and stealing on your behalf for weeks, burning the villages of all of your enemies in the North."

The king was horrified. "But I have no enemies in the North," he said.

"Well," said the knight, "you do now."

South Africa, 1885. A couple of days before Rorkes Drift. One hundred British soldiers are surrounded by 100,000 Zulus. It has been a long hot day and dusk is falling. General Lord Chinless Wonder turns to his batman and says, "Corporal, it's too quiet. The natives are up to something and our relieving forces are still two days away."

Right on cue, the sound of a chant, gradually rising, can be heard. Slowly but surely it reaches an ear-splitting intensity; 100,000 Zulus are belting out their challenge – the prelude to battle. Just as the soldiers think they can stand it no more, the chanting completely ceases. The absolute silence is almost deafening now that the Zulus are hushed.

Then the sound of war drums begins and gathers tempo gradually until it seems to be coming from everywhere at once. Once again the general turns to his loyal servant. "Corporal, I don't like the sound of those drums."

At which point a Zulu pops up from behind a bush 50 yards away and says, "He's not our regular drummer."

In days of old, when knights were bold, one particular knight was leaving for a crusade and called one of his squires. "I'm leaving for the crusade. Here is the key to my wife's chastity belt. If, in ten years, I haven't returned, you may use the key, as I'm sure she will have needs."

The knight sets out on the dusty road, armoured from head to toe. He takes one last look at his castle and sees the squire rushing across the drawbridge, yelling, "Stop! Stop! Thank goodness I was able to catch you. This is the wrong key."

A trio of former soldiers were bragging about the heroic exploits of their ancestors one afternoon down at the Legion.

"My great-grandfather, at age 13, was a drummer boy at the Charge of the Light Brigade," declares one proudly.

"Mine won the Victoria Cross at Ypres," boasts another.

"I'm the only soldier in my family," confessed vet number three, "but if my great-grandfather was living today, he'd be the most famous man in the world."

"Really? What did he do?" his friends wanted to know.

"Nothing much. But he would be 165 years old."

At his medical a conscripted soldier visited the optometrist:

"Can you read this writing?" asked the doctor.

"No," replied his charge.

"Move a little closer. And now?"

"No."

"Ok – move forward a few steps. Now try."

"Sorry, still no."

"Right-ho. Walk forward until you can read it?"

The soldier-to-be approaches the chart and peers at it.

"OK. Now, I see it. It says 'if you can read this you are fit for bayonet fighting!'"

King Arthur was preparing for an expedition that would keep him away from Camelot for some time. He was worried about leaving Queen Guinevere alone with all of the Knights of the Round Table, so he went to Merlin for advice.

The wizard looked thoughtful, and said that he would see if he could come up with something, and asked the King to come back in a week.

A week later, King Arthur was back in Merlin's laboratory where the good wizard showed him his latest invention. It was a chastity belt, except that it had a rather large hole in the most obvious place. "This is no good, Merlin!" the King exclaimed. "Look at this opening. How is this supposed to protect the Queen's honour?"

"Ah, sire, just observe," said Merlin as he searched his cluttered workbench until he found what he was looking for: an old, worn-out wand. He inserted it into the gaping aperture of the chastity belt whereupon a small guillotine blade came down and cut it neatly in two.

"Merlin, you are a genius!" said the grateful monarch. "Now I can leave, knowing that my Queen is fully protected."

After putting Guinevere in the device, King Arthur then set out upon his Quest. Several years passed until he returned to Camelot.

Immediately, he assembled all of his knights in the courtyard and had them drop their trousers for an informal 'short arm' inspection. Sure enough! Each and every one of them was either amputated or damaged in some way. All of them except Sir Galahad.

"Sir Galahad," exclaimed King Arthur, "the one and only true knight! Only you among all the nobles have been true to me. What is it in my power to grant you? Name it and it is yours!"

But Sir Galahad was speechless…

Julius Caesar was addressing the crowd in the Coliseum. "Friends, Romans, Countrymen, lend me your ears. Tomorrow I take our glorious army to conquer Gaul. We shall kill many Gauls and return victorious."

The crowd rose to their feet "Yeeeeeeeeeeeeeeeeeeeeees! Hail, mighty Caesar!"

Brutus turned to his mate and said, "He doesn't half talk some shite, eh? He couldn't fight his way out of a wet parchment bag."

Six months later, Caesar returned, having conquered Gaul, and addressed the crowd in the Coliseum. "Friends, Romans, Countrymen, I have returned from our campaign in Gaul and as I promised, we killed 50,000 Gauls."

The crowd rose to their feet again. "Yeeeeeeeeeeeeeeeeeeeees! Hail, mighty Caesar!"

Brutus once again turned to his mate. "I'm sick of his bullshit, I'm off to Gaul to check this out." So Brutus set off for Gaul and three weeks later returned to Rome.

Caesar was addressing the public in the Coliseum again. "Friends, Romans, Countrymen, tomorrow we set off for Britain and we are going to sort those bastards out."

The crowd rose to their feet. "Yeeeeeeeeeeeeeeeeeeeeeeeeeeeees! Hail, mighty Caesar!"

Brutus jumped up and shouted, "Caesar, you are a liar. You told us that you had killed 50,000 Gauls, but I've been to check it out and you only killed 25,000!"

The crowd was stunned and all sat down in silence. Caesar got up and looked slowly round the Coliseum then across at Brutus and said, "Brutus, you are forgetting one thing… away Gauls count double in Europe."

THE BIG ONES
- WORLD WARS

IF WORLD WAR I WAS A BAR FIGHT...

Germany, Austria and Italy are standing together in the middle of a pub when Serbia bumps into Austria and spills Austria's pint. Austria demands Serbia buy him a completely new suit because there are splashes on its trouser leg. Germany expresses his support for Austria's point of view. Britain recommends that everyone calm down a bit. Serbia points out that he can't afford a whole suit, but offers to pay for the cleaning of Austria's trousers. Russia and Serbia look at Austria. Austria asks Serbia, "Who are you looking at?" Russia suggests that Austria should leave his little brother alone. Austria enquires as to whose army will assist Russia in compelling him to do so?

Germany appeals to Britain that France has been "looking at him" and that this is sufficiently out of order that Britain should intervene. Britain replies that "France can look at who he wants to, Britain is looking at Germany too, and what is Germany going to do about it?" Germany tells Russia to "stop looking" at Austria, or Germany will render Russia incapable of such action. Britain and France ask Germany whether he's looking at Belgium. Turkey and Germany go off into a corner and whisper. When they come back, Turkey makes a show of not looking at anyone.

Germany rolls up his sleeves, looks at France, and punches Belgium. France and Britain punch Germany. Austria punches Russia. Germany punches Britain and France with one hand and Russia with the other. Russia throws a punch at Germany, but misses and nearly falls over. Japan calls over from the other side of the room that it's on Britain's side, but stays on that side. Italy surprises everyone by punching Austria. Australia punches Turkey, and gets punched back. There are no hard feelings because Britain made Australia do it. France gets thrown through a plate-glass window, but gets back up and carries on fighting. Russia gets thrown through another window, gets knocked out, suffers brain damage, and wakes up with a complete personality change.

Italy throws a punch at Austria and misses, but Austria falls over anyway. Italy raises both fists in the air and runs round the room chanting. America waits until Germany is about to fall over from sustained punching from Britain and France, then walks over and smashes him with a bar stool, pretending that he won the fight all by itself. By now all of the chairs are broken and the big mirror over the bar is shattered. Britain, France and America agree that Germany threw the first punch, so the whole thing is Germany's fault. While Germany is still unconscious, they go through its pockets, steal its wallet, and buy drinks for all of their friends.

Two young privates were going into the trenches for the first time, and their captain promised them 10 shillings for every German they killed. Jimmy lay down to rest, and Tommy performed the duty of watching. Jimmy had not lain long when he was awakened by Tommy shouting,

"They're coming!"

"Who's coming?" shouted Jimmy.

"The Germans," replied Tommy.

"How many are there?"

"About fifty thousand."

"Blimey," shouted Jimmy, jumping up and grabbing his rifle. "We're going to make a fucking fortune!"

It is late 1940. Hitler has called Mussolini on the phone:

"Benito, aren't you in Athens yet?" the Fuhrer barks angrily.

"I can't hear you, Adolf," replies the Italian dictator.

Hitler, now irritated, repeats, "I said, haven't your feeble armies made it to Athens yet?"

"I can't hear you," shouts Mussolini. "You must be ringing from a long way off. Presumably you're in London?"

Mick O'Riordan was a legend in World War I. He was the most famous sniper in the history of warfare. The list of his victims was hundreds of names' long, and yet his system was so simple. He would work out that ninety per cent of Germans were called Hans. So Mick would lie in no man's land, settle in a shell hole, set up the rifle and call: "Hello, Hans, are you there?"

A German head would rise up and shout, "Ja!" whereupon O'Riordan would shoot him.

This worked very well for many months until he came across an equally smart German sniper. This man had worked out that over fifty per cent of Irishmen were called Mick, so he tried the same plan. There he lay, directly opposite O'Riordan, and called out: "Are you there, Mick?"

"Yes," said O'Riordan without moving. "Is that you, Hans?"

The German rose up and said, "Ja!" and Mick shot him…

I was at a party the other night, listening to a bloke going on and on, complaining about the status of some of Britain's most renowned figures in history…

"I mean," he went on. "Isn't it damning that some of the kids today don't recognise the name of Britain's greatest ever leader? Take the man who defeated the Nazis, the man who is regarded as one of the great wartime leaders, who is considered a magnificent orator, an accomplished historian and a successful writer to boot. Isn't it absolutely awful that when they hear the name 'Churchill', they think of a dog selling insurance?"

Unfortunately, I found myself nodding and saying, "Ohhhhhh yes!"

OLD WORLD WAR II SAYING:

"When the British shoot, the Germans duck, when the Germans shoot, the British duck, when the Americans shoot, everybody ducks…"

During World War II, selective service wasn't always so selective. My near-sighted friend went before the draft board to explain just how poor his vision was. "If I lose my glasses, I won't be able to see at all," he told them.

"Don't you worry," replied the sergeant in charge. "When we attack, we'll stick you in front of the battalion. You won't miss a thing."

"Private, you are the worst shot I've ever seen!" said the corpora

"Does that mean I won't be going to the front?" asked the private, hopefully.

"No, lad," said the corporal. "It means you won't be coming back."

Two soldiers from the a front line regiment had found a haversack in the captured German trench and were carrying it back to their own lines.

"What's inside it?" asked Jimmy.

"Three hand grenades," said Tommy.

"In the name of God – what happens if one goes off?" screamed Jimmy.

"No problem" said Tommy. "we'll tell the sergeant we only found two!"

A true story tells of a naval flotilla preparing to leave Liverpool on convoy escort duty.

Unusually, this flotilla included a submarine among its number. The submarine captain sent the following signal to the flotilla commander:

"In the event of attack, I intend to remain on the surface."

The flotilla commander replied: "So do I."

London. World War II. A fireman had just rescued a lady from her damaged house after a bombing raid. The local press asked if her husband was in the house. She replied, "No, he is in Libya fighting... the bloody coward!"

The general had barely arrived in the forward area when a sniper's bullet removed a button from his shirt. He threw himself to the ground in terror but the men stood around with the greatest unconcern. The general yelled at a passing sergeant, "Hey, isn't somebody going to kill that damned sniper?"

The sergeant looked down at the general and replied, "I guess not, General. We're scared that, if we kill him, the enemy will replace him with somebody who really knows how to shoot."

Two pensioners were sitting on a park bench talking about the Great War.

"Do you remember those pills they gave us to keep our minds off those French girls?"

"Come to think of it, I do," replied his mate.

"Well I think mine are beginning to work!"

An English prisoner of war has sustained some nasty injuries and the German medic tells him, "Englander, your arm is infected with gangrene. We must cut it off."

The stoic Englishman says, "Could you possibly drop it over England when you go bombing."

The medic replies, "Ja, no problem."

A few weeks later the medic tells the Englishman that they will have to cut his other arm off. The Englishman says, "Well, it would be really nice of you chaps if you could drop it over England like you did last time."

"Ja, we can do that," says the German.

The next day the medic tells him that they will have to cut his leg off. Once again the Brit says, "Well, would you be so good as to do the same as before?"

The German replies, "Ja. OK, Tommy."

The following day the German tells him that they have to cut off his other leg. "Well," begins the Brit, "Could you just…" The German snaps, "No! Enough!. Now we think you are trying to escape!"

An Australian finds himself next to a British soldier in the trenches. The British soldier turns to him and says, "Good to see you, mate. Have you come here to die?"

To which the Australian replies, "No, mate, I arrived yesterday!"

In the trenches allied troops are hemmed in by the Germans and awaiting orders via a carrier pigeon. They see the pigeon approaching with a message but then the bird falls out of the sky.

The captain asks for a volunteer to go and retrieve the message from the pigeon. Eventually Archie steps forward.

He says, "I'll go for my country." He crawls out of the trench and all he can hear are bullets, mortars, and bombs. Everyone assumes that Archie is dead. Two hours later Archiearrives back into the trench and everyone cheers his safe return.

The captain asks, "Did you get to the pigeon?"

Archie says, "Yes."

The captain says, "Did it have a message?"

Archie says, "Yes."

The captain says, "What was the message?"

Archie says, "Coo! Coo!"

A World War I general is giving his eve-of-battle pep talk. "Now, men," he says. "It's important to remember the two main differences between a battle and manoeuvres. Can any soldier here tell me what they are?"

A squaddie in the front row pipes up first. "There is a real enemy, sir."

The general replies, "Good man. And who can tell me the second?"

From the back row comes a muffled yell. "I can. There are no generals, sir."

An old Englishman lands at Charles de Gaulle Airport in Paris and approaches a very short-tempered French customs officer. The Frenchman grumpily asks the old chap for his passport. As the old man fumbles around, the Frenchman snaps at him that he is holding up the line and asks him if he has ever been to France before.

As the old man rummages through his bag, he replies, "Yes, I have."

The angry customs officer says, "In that case, you should know to have your passport ready to show to a French customs officer."

The old man takes a slow breath, then looks up at the burly jobsworth.

"Listen, Monsieur," he says slowly and clearly. "When I came to France last time – I didn't have a passport."

The customs officer looks back at him disbelievingly. So the old timer continued, "And even if I did I have one, there were certainly no Frenchmen around to check it in 1944."

The German air traffic controllers at Frankfurt Airport are known for being a bad-tempered lot. They not only expect one to know one's gate parking location, but how to get there without any assistance from them. But one ex-RAF pilot (now flying a British Airways 747, call sign: Ironbird 056) was not prepared to take any nonsense...

Ironbird 056:

"Hello, Frankfurt. Ironbird 056 clear of active runway."

Ground Control:

"Ironbird 056. Taxi to gate Alpha One-Seven."

Ground Control:

"Ironbird 056, do you not know where you are going?"

Ironbird 056:

"Stand by, Ground, I'm looking up our gate location now."

Ground Control (impatient): "Ironbird 056, have you not been to Frankfurt before?"

Ironbird 056 (coolly):

"Yes, Ground, twice – in 1944. But it was dark… and I didn't land."

During an argument with my granddad, he screamed,

"You'd be speaking German if it wasn't for me!"

I said, "Hang on, you didn't fight in the war."

"I know that," he replied. "But I was the one who told you to choose French for your languages GCSE, remember?"

In no man's land at the Battle of the Somme, a small British raiding party left their trenches to scout the terrain. There in the mud they spotted a head with a steel helmet sticking out of the mud.

"Hello there," called the lieutenant. "Who are you?"

"I'm Corporal Dunstan, sir," came a shrill voice. "I'm a member of the 17th Cavalry Regiment, and I've got myself stuck in this mud and I'm sinking fast!"

"Don't worry, lad," called the officer. "We'll soon get you free."

With that, the soldiers looped a rope around themselves, fastened it to a tree and crawled out to lever Dunstan from the mud. Muscles bulging and eyes popping, they pulled his head, his neck, his ears, anything they could grab hold of. They heaved until his shoulders started to come free, but by now they were almost exhausted.

"Sir," said Dunstan, "Do you think it would help if I took me feet out of the stirrups?"

There's a young soldier in the World War I who can take no more of the gassing and the brutality and watching his mates die one after the other. The lad throws down his weapon, turns his back on the enemy and runs. He doesn't look back, but runs on through his exhaustion until, eventually, the sound of battle is no longer even a distant hum. Then he falls to the ground and sleeps.

When he wakes he sees in front of him, on the earth, a pair of highly polished officer's boots, and he hears a booming voice coming from above.

"What are you doing here?"

"Oh, I'm sorry, Major," says the lad. "I couldn't take any more. I watched my friends being shot, I saw them being gassed, it was carnage. It was terrible. I just ran and ran. I'm sorry, Major, I'm really sorry.'

"I'm not a major," says the voice. "I'm a general."

"Oh, my God," says the young deserter. "I didn't think I had run that far.'

In Nazi Germany, if you spelt the name Hitler incorrectly you'd get a visit from the Ges-typo.

During World War II, an American warship was attacked by the Japanese. A torpedo was heading towards the ship and a hit seemed inevitable. So the captain told the navigator to go down to the crew quarters and tell a joke or something – at least they would die laughing.

The navigator went down and said to the crew, "What would you think if I split the whole ship in two by hitting my dick against the table?" The crew burst laughing. So the navigator pulled his dick out and whammed it on the table. Just when the dick hit the table, a huge explosion tore the ship apart. The only survivors were the captain and the navigator.

As they floated around in a lifeboat, the captain asked the navigator, "Well, the crew really laughed. What did you tell them?" The navigator told him what he'd said.

The captain replied, "Well, you'd better be careful with that dick of yours. The torpedo missed!"

If the Nazis had won the war, would we be being sold insurance by a dog called Hitler?

During World War II, Richard Wynn, on flight duty with the 8th Air Force Division in Europe, was shot down and captured by the Germans. After a year as a prisoner of war, he escaped and made his way back to his bomber group in England. One of his first acts there was to find the corporal on duty in the parachute building.

"Corporal," he said. "A year ago I had occasion to use one of the parachutes that your men had packed and I want you to know how delighted I was to find it in perfect working order. I give you my deepest compliments and appreciation."

"You know, Lieutenant, it's a funny thing," the corporal replied. "In this line of work, we never get any complaints."

Johnny joined the Home Guard during World War II and was given a rifle, ammunition and a very important task.

"I want you to guard the town against insurgents," said the captain. "We've got a curfew in force. Anyone out of doors after midnight is to be shot on sight!"

There stood Johnny at the town square, ever alert, when suddenly a figure came out of the darkness. "Who goes there?" he called.

"It's only Larry the greengrocer," came the answer.

Bang! Johnny shot the man down.

"Good shot," said the captain, "but it's only eleven thirty."

"Yes," said Johnny, "but I know where he lives and he would never have made it home in time!"

Two Tommys dug in in Flanders during World War I had been stuck in a trench for three days when one says, "I can't wait any longer. I'm desperate for a shit."

"Well, you can't go in here," says his mate. "It's really going to stink. There's another trench over there. I'll cover you and when you are finished just give me a shout and I'll cover your arse and make sure you get back safely."

"OK." So the private runs across under cover of his comrade. His mate waits for five, then ten, and finally, twenty minutes before becoming really concerned. He shouts out but gets no reply. Finally more than an hour later he hears his mate calling, "Cover me, I'm coming back."

When he jumps back into the trench, his mate says, "Where the fuck have you been? You've been gone for over an hour."

"Yeah, I'm sorry but there was a girl over there," replied the Tommy. "I played with her tits, fondled her arse, turned her round and took her from behind!"

"You lucky bastard," said the other. "And I bet you even got a blow job, didn't you?"

"Nah," said the other, disappointedly. "She didn't have a head."

World War II found my dad being posted to North Africa – and he had never been further than the Isle of Wight before. Apparently he got on board the troopship and asked one of the crew where the gents' were. The navy lad replied, "Port side, mate."

"Jesus!" replied my old man. "We won't be there for another three weeks!"

Little Jimmy goes to see his granddad, to ask him about his experiences of the War for a school history project. After talking for ten minutes, Granddad can see that Johnny is bored. So to liven things up, he says, "If you promise not to tell your grandmother and keep quiet, I'll show you a bullet!"

"Wow," says Jimmy. "You've got a real bullet?"

So Granddad shows little Jimmy the bullet. After carefully inspecting it he turns to the old man and says, "Do you have any other souvenirs, Granddad?"

The old man smiles and tells him, "I've got a revolver."

"A REVOL…"

"SShhh! Jimmy, don't let your grandmother hear," whispers Granddad.

"Sorry, Granddad," replies the boy. "I was excited. Where do you keep the revolver?"

"In my old artillery box with the grenades," smiles Granddad.

"GREN…" squeals the boy.

"Hush, lad," the old man warns. "Your grandmother won't be happy about me showing you weapons."

"Can I see the grenades?"

"Yes," answers the old chap, pleased that his grandson is so interested, but still wary of his wife. "I suppose you'll want to see the rifle too."

"A rifle!" breathes the boy. "Oh, Granddad, where is the rifle?"

"With the machine gun," confesses the old man.

"A MACH… machine gun, Granddad?" the boy states incredulously. "Where's the machine gun?"

The old man looks up and replies, "In the loft behind the tank…"

"A FUCKING TANK!"

Two builders are sitting high up on a New York skyscraper scaffolding when one of them suddenly stands up, steps off the building and plummets to his death.

The foreman races up and demands to know why the other builder jumped.

"Dunno, boss," he says. "We were talking about what our fathers did during World War II and I told him that mine flew in Wellingtons over Germany."

Is it right that the World War I soldier who survived mustard gas and pepper spray could be referred to as 'a seasoned veteran'?

A British officer and a Gurkha soldier are attacked by a Japanese patrol and have no time to fire their weapons. The Gurkha soldier rushes forward and, in a whirl of movement, draws his kukri and quickly decapitates most of the enemy, leaving one standing stock still.

"I say, Rambahadur, that's pretty impressive stuff, but you've missed one," says the British officer.

"No, just wait until he shakes his head."

A Jewish man is watching a TV documentary in a New York bar. He's getting more and more drunk and has his head propped in his hands as he watches the TV telling all about the Japanese attack on Pearl Harbor. The narrator says, "On 7th December 1941, the Imperial Japanese Navy launched an unprovoked air attack on Pearl Harbor in Hawaii."

The man tuts angrily into his beer.

"A third of the US Fleet was destroyed in the single worst attack of the Second World War."

The man gets redder and tuts even more loudly.

"Twenty-five thousand US men and women were killed that day, some of them burned horrifically!"

The Jewish guy turns round and sees a little Asian guy on a stool at the end of the bar. He runs over and punches the Asian in the face, knocking him off his stool. The Asian man shouts, "What the hell did you do that for?"

"That was for Pearl Harbor!" proclaims his assailant, feeling proud of himself. But the Asian fellow replies, "For God's sake, that was the fuckin' Japanese, I'm Taiwanese!"

To which the Jewish man says, "Japanese, Chinese, Taiwanese, you're all the same!" He sits back on his stool and starts drinking his beer.

The Taiwanese sits back on his stool, growling to himself. In a moment, he goes charging across the bar and plants a flying kick on the side of the American Jew's head, sending him crashing into the wall, with a 'Thud!'

"Now what are you doing?" cries the injured American. "That was for the Titanic!"

"What are you on about? That was an iceberg!"

"Goldberg, Weinberg, Iceberg – you're all the fucking same!"

IF WORLD WAR II WAS A BAR FIGHT...

After the last bar fight, America has got the job of running the bar. Germany finally gets out of hospital and goes back in only to find everyone drinking with his money.

Austria is sitting happily in the corner by himself. But Germany goes and plonks himself next to him and won't stop bothering him. A minute later, Germany's grabbed Czechoslovakia and busies himself irritating Czechoslovakia too.

On the other side of the room, Japan has been drinking all day, building up the courage to punch China. Finally Japan gets round to landing one on his bitter enemy, but bartender America tells them to knock it off.

Britain has spotted Germany bullying Austria and Czechoslovakia and has a word. Germany nods and even signs a beer mat promising that he won't bother anybody else. As soon as Britain goes to show his mates the beer mat, Germany socks Poland – claiming that Poland is laughing at him. Russia sees what happens and goes to intervene – giving Poland a kicking too.

Germany turns to Britain and France, who are standing in the middle of the room and making an 'if-you-think-you're-hard-enough' gesture and says, "I'll take you all on, come on, then." But Britain and France slink back to their table and continue to utter threats in low voices. Denmark, Norway, Holland and Belgium, who popped in for a quick one after work, all look worried, finish their drinks in a hurry and yell for the bill.

Finland, who has been sitting in a corner quietly, notices Russia is distracted going through the unconscious Poland's pockets, and quickly sneaks up behind and smashes a vodka bottle over Russia's head. Semi-concussed Russia mistakes Germany for their best friend and gives them a hearty bear hug.

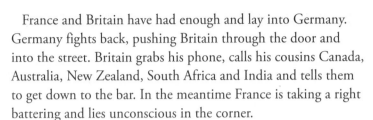

France and Britain have had enough and lay into Germany. Germany fights back, pushing Britain through the door and into the street. Britain grabs his phone, calls his cousins Canada, Australia, New Zealand, South Africa and India and tells them to get down to the bar. In the meantime France is taking a right battering and lies unconscious in the corner.

Britain finally walks back in to find Germany buying a drink for Italy and everyone else staring into their pints, making out they're not there. In a corner booth, Bulgaria, Hungary and Romania stand up and declare that Germany and Italy are their new best mates and buy them a round.

In come Britain's cousins and the whole thing kicks off. While everybody is looking distracted, Japan puts China into a headlock and begins punching his head. America tells Japan to knock it off and that he's had too much to drink and is banned.

Japan jumps over the bar and punches America.

America the bartender is furious, grabbing his baseball bat and leaping over the bar to plough in. Russia comes round and realises that Germany isn't his best mate after all, and changes sides. As Italy runs and hides in the loo, Germany is pinned to the wall by Russia while America pummels him with the baseball bat and Britain kicks him in the bollocks.

The barman then goes for Japan, smashing his kneecaps with the bat. As Japan lies groaning on the bar room floor, America nips back behind the bar, fetches his Colt 45 and shoots Japan twice in the heart.

During World War II, the Germans would come into occupied villages to steal the food and ravage the women. They arrived at one particular village in Poland to find word had got out and everyone had already left. They made themselves at home in the deserted hamlet, before coming across one terrified young man.

"Bring us some food," they demanded of him.

The young man says, "The villagers have taken everything, I have only half a loaf of bread left."

"War is war, bring us the bread."

So he fetches the last of his food.

"Bring us some wine!" They then order.

"But I doubt if there is any in the house, you know how things are these days!"

"War is war," comes the retort, "bring us the wine."

The young man searches the village and manages to find half a bottle and gives it to them.

"Now, bring us a woman," the commander says with a grin.

"But everyone has left the village. The only woman left here is my ninety-year-old grandmother!"

"War is war, bring her to us."

The old woman is brought forward and she's so haggard and diseased that the soldiers decide against it. "OK, sonny," says the disappointed commander. "We'll let you off this time."

"The hell you will," says the grandmother. "War is war!"

Hitler went to a fortune teller to find out what day he would die. The fortune teller arsed around with Tarot cards and a crystal ball for a bit before saying, "You will die on a Jewish holiday."

Hitler was not particularly pleased to hear this, but he asked, "Which Jewish holiday?"

The fortune teller said, "Whatever day you die will be a Jewish holiday."

Three British pilots were captured by Germans in World War II. The Gestapo came up with a devious way to make the pilots crack and reveal what they knew. They made them stand at attention, turn their heads from side to side and say, "Tick tock" over and over.

After about three hours, the first pilot cracked and started telling all he knew, signing everything they put in front of him. An hour later, the second pilot cracked and gave away the top secret plans he had sworn to take to his death.

The third pilot was defiant. He would only turn his head to one side and just say, "Tick… Tick… Tick…" This method enabled him to withstand their pressure.

The Gestapo officer was furious. He put his face into the airman's face and shouted, "You thinks you are zo schmart, Englische swinehund! But I'm telling you… vee haf vays of making you TOCK!"

An old sailor and an old soldier were in the pub arguing about who had had the tougher career.

"I was in the army for thirty years," the soldier declared proudly. "I fought for my country around the world. I was just a teenager when I fought with Monty at Al Alamein where we dug into foxholes for days, with scorpions biting our legs and Rommel pounding us with mortars. Two years later I hit the beach at Normandy. I crawled up the bloodstained beach and took out an entire enemy machine-gun-nest with a single grenade. Then, as a sergeant, I fought in Korea at the Battle of the Imjin River, where, completely outnumbered, we sustained a barrage of artillery and small-arms fire, but held our positions for three days, fighting off the enemy with bayonets when our ammo ran out."

"Ah," said the sailor with a dismissive wave of his hand, "lucky bastard. All shore duty, huh?"

An tourist went to Portsmouth to see Nelson's flagship *HMS Victory*. On the tour of the ship, the guide pointed out a raised brass plaque on the deck.

"That's where Nelson fell," said the guide.

The tourist was unimpressed. "I'm not surprised," he said. "I nearly tripped on the thing myself."

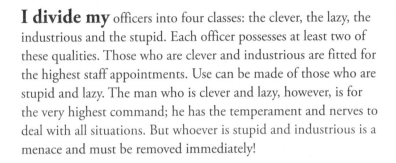

I divide my officers into four classes: the clever, the lazy, the industrious and the stupid. Each officer possesses at least two of these qualities. Those who are clever and industrious are fitted for the highest staff appointments. Use can be made of those who are stupid and lazy. The man who is clever and lazy, however, is for the very highest command; he has the temperament and nerves to deal with all situations. But whoever is stupid and industrious is a menace and must be removed immediately!

General Baron Kurt von Hammerstein-Equord
Commander-in-Chief
The Reichswehr

Mrs Irene Graham of Thorpe Avenue, Boscombe, delighted the audience with her reminiscence of the German prisoner of war who was sent each week to tend her garden. He was repatriated at the end of 1945, she recalled. "He had always seemed a nice friendly chap, but when the crocuses came up in the middle of our lawn in February 1946, they spelt out 'Heil Hitler."

Bournemouth Evening Echo

If you really think old soldiers fade away, you should watch one trying to get into an old uniform.

MODERN
CONFLICT

THE PLAN

The modern fighting force needs to be a well-oiled machine where each cog knows exactly what to do and what it is contributing. For this reason, detailed plans are drawn up for each arm of the services. So how come everything doesn't always go to plan?

Infantry. Hasn't got the concentration span to actually read the whole Plan, but takes it very seriously indeed. Produces laminated copies of the Plan and distributes it to every man (sergeants carry spare plans just in case).

Parachute Regiment. Plans are for Hats. Insists on deploying first on any operation that appears, so everyone else can have whatever plan they want. Jumps, lands in wrong place, takes 50% casualties in ankle injuries and realises that it's left ammunition back in Colchester.

Cavalry. Looks at the Plan but, on seeing arrows, realises the Plan involves a degree of navigation alien to cavalry manoeuvres. Opts to drive off at speed to the track sheds and have impromptu Pimms parties.

Royal Marines Commandos. Pretends to be very laid back about the Plan, talking about drinking and getting naked instead. But secretly gets very competitive about the Plan, insisting that the Plan can only work with commandos because it requires poise, reach and hoofing wets.

AGC (Adjutant General's Corps). Receives the plan in an envelope, opens it and sticks it at bottom of huge pile of paperwork.

Combat Engineers. Likes plans. Takes the Plan and adds whole new sections, with diagrams no one else understands or cares about. Still adding new bits when the Plan changes, at which point the previous work becomes irrelevant. Has a huff and blames Chieftain chassis for not allowing engineers to keep up with the pace of everyone else's thinking.

Artillery. Also likes plans. Makes very detailed plans, with numbers, timings and smoke. Talks a lot about HE, smoke and last safe moments. Whatever the Plan actually entails, just keep firing all guns until the ammo runs out.

Special Forces. Writes the Plan in pencil on the back of ciggie packet and makes sure no one else has a clue what the Plan is. Ensures that the Special Forces Plan is different from the one everyone else is working to and checks that it will make a suitable story for exaggeration after leaving the service. Places tape over eyes, can't see the Plan any longer and gets captured by locals – providing ideal material for the novel.

REME (Royal Electrical and Mechanical Engineers). Happy to see the Plan, but disturbed by the lack of attention to health and safety issues. Places a yellow warning sign in front of the Plan – which everyone trips over.

RAF. Likes plans. Takes the Plan into cockpit, but is distracted by an invite to Prince William's party and forgets about the Plan completely. Flies back and complains about noisy air-conditioning in the hotel room and the lack of streaky bacon on the breakfast menu.

The Ministry of Defence were considering cheaper options on submarine designs. Someone submitted the idea of a submarine made out of polystyrene. It didn't go down very well.

MILITARY TRUISMS

- When the pin is pulled, Mr Grenade is no longer our friend.

- No plan survives the first contact intact.

- Cluster bombing is very, very accurate. The bombs always hit the ground.

- Whoever said the pen is mightier than the sword obviously never encountered automatic weapons.

- Any ship can be a minesweeper... once.

- If the enemy is in range, so are you.

- The enemy invariably attacks on either of two occasions: when they're ready or when you're not.

- The quartermaster has only two sizes: too large and too small.

- If it's stupid but works, it isn't stupid.

- No combat-ready unit has ever passed inspection.

- Professional soldiers are predictable, but the world is full of amateurs.

- If your attack is going well, it is an ambush.

- Military Intelligence is an oxymoron.

In 2010, the world's daftest soldiers reportedly stormed a department store in London. Having shot up the soft furnishings section and caused chaos locally, they later stated that, despite US claims, they had still reason to believe that they were holding Summer Bed Linen.

Q: Why can't anyone count exactly how many soldiers there still are in Afghanistan?

A: It's because of the tally ban.

Q: Why don't they let circumcised men into Sandhurst?

A: Because you have to be a complete prick to be an officer.

A new arrival at the British base in Gereshk, Helmand Province, asked the lads about the local girls. They told him that there weren't any. However, on a Friday night the local tribe leader would let you have a go at one of his camels for ten Afghani.

Come Friday night, the lads are all getting their deodorant and hair gel out. "What's all this in aid of?" asked the newcomer.

The rest stared at him until one replied, "You don't want one of the ugly fuckers, do you?"

Just back in Blighty, a junior officer had visited his local GP.

"But doctor," protested the soldier, "it's impossible for my wife to be pregnant. I've been posted in Afghanistan for the last year – I haven't been back home in all that time."

"I'm sorry," said the doctor, "but that's what we in the medical profession call a grudge pregnancy."

"What's that?" asked the unfortunate squaddie.

"I'm afraid that someone had it in for you."

A blast today covered central London in glue.
Police reports suggest terrorists have set off a NoMoreNails bomb.

CNN have film of what they believe is a mortar attack by the Forces in Afghanistan. Four men are seen throwing two buckets of sand and one bucket of cement over the wall of a Taliban position.

In July 2012, Britain received the first of the state-of-the-art F-35 stealth fighter jets from US manufacturer Lockheed Martin. It came complete with a bumper sticker saying: 'If you can read this, we've wasted £100 million!'

A guard is on patrol, bored and cold, when he hears a booming voice from the heavens.

"DIG, SOLDIER!" says the voice.

The soldier looks around, a little confused.

"DIG!" booms the voice, once again.

The guard thinks, "Well, I've nothing better to do" and starts digging the sand in front of him. Suddenly he hits a wooden box. He picks it up and the voice shouts, "OPEN, SOLDIER!"

He opens it to see hundreds of gold coins. He's just beginning to think about all of the things that he could buy when he's shocked to hear the voice shout again.

"CASINO!"

At this point the soldier realises he's on to something special. He leaves his post and heads for the local casino. He is hardly through the casino door when he hears the voice shout:

"ROULETTE!"

So, he walks over to the roulette table and listens out for his next instruction.

"16 BLACK!" the voice says.

The man puts the whole chest on 16 Black. The wheel is spun and it lands on 5 Red.

"OH FUCK!" shouts the voice…

A *Times* journalist, a BBC reporter and an SAS sergeant were all captured by terrorists in Iraq. The leader of the terrorists told them that he would grant them each one last request before they were beheaded.

The journalist said, "Well, I'm from Yorkshire, so I'd like a nice pint of bitter." The leader nodded to an underling who left and returned with the beer. The journalist drank it and said, "OK. Now I can die content."

The BBC reporter said, "I'm a reporter to the end. I want to take out my tape recorder and describe the scene here and what's about to happen. Maybe someday someone will hear it and know that I was a professional right through to the end." The leader directed his junior to hand over the tape recorder and the reporter filed her piece. She then said, "OK. My report is done. Now I can die happy that I have done my job."

The leader turned and said, "And now, Mr tough guy, what is your final wish?"

"Kick me," said the soldier.

"What?" asked the leader? "Will you mock us in your last hour?"

"No, I'm not joking. I want you to kick me," insisted the SAS man. So the leader and his junior gave him a good kicking.

The soldier went sprawling, but rolled, pulled a 9mm from under his flak jacket and came up shooting, killing the leader. In the resulting confusion, he snatched the terrorist's automatic and sprayed his captors with gunfire. In an instant, all the terrorists were either dead or fleeing for their lives.

As the soldier was untying the other two, they asked him, "Why didn't you just shoot them straight away? Why on earth did you ask them to kick you first?"

"What?" replied the soldier. "And have you two hacks report that I was the aggressor!"

LAWS OF SURVIVAL:

- Don't ever be the first, don't ever be the last, and don't ever volunteer to do anything that suppressive fire won't.

- Always bear in mind that 'friendly fire' isn't.

- If you find yourself in a fair fight, you didn't plan your mission properly.

- Don't draw fire; it irritates the people around you.

- Try to look unimportant, because the bad guys may be low on ammo.

- If you are short of everything except enemy, you are in combat.

- When you have secured an area, do not forget to tell the enemy.

- Remember, tracers work both ways.

- Incoming fire has the right-of-way.

- Make it too tough for the enemy to get in, and you can't get out.

- Flying is better than walking. Walking is better than running. Running is better than crawling. All of these, however, are better than extraction by a Med-Evac.

During the Iraq War, President Bush was receiving his daily briefing. His aide concludes the meeting by saying: "Finally, Mr President, I have to inform you that three Brazilian soldiers were killed in Basra yesterday."

"Oh no!" the President exclaims. "That's terrible!"

His staff sit stunned at this display of emotion, nervously watching as the President sits, head in hands.

Finally, the President looks up and asks, "Exactly how many is a 'Brazillion' again?"

A Soldier stationed in Belize wrote to his wife to ask her to send him a harmonica to occupy his free time and keep his mind off the local women. The wife complied and sent the best one she could find, along with a dozen tuition books.

Rotated back home, he rushed to their house and through the front door. "Oh, darling," he gushed. "Come here… let me look at you…let me hold you! Let's have a fine dinner out, then make love all night. I've missed your loving so much!"

The wife, keeping her distance, said, "All in good time, lover. First, let's hear you play that harmonica."

BEEP... CLICK...

Thank you for calling the British Army. I'm sorry, but all of our units are out at the moment, or are otherwise engaged. Please leave a message with the name of your country, name of organisation, the region, the specific crisis and a number at which we can call you. As soon as we have sorted out Afghanistan, Kosovo, Bosnia, Macedonia, Iraq, Northern Ireland, Sierra Leone, the Congo, played security guards at the Olympic Games and marched up and down in front of the Queen, we will return your call.

Please speak after the tone or, if you require more options, listen to the following:

- If your crisis is small and close to the sea, press 1 for the Royal Marines.

- If your concern is distant, with a tropical climate, good hotels and can be solved by one or two low-risk bombing runs, please press 2 for the Royal Air Force. (Please note that this service is not available after 16:30 or at weekends.)

- If your enquiry concerns a situation which can be resolved by a warship, some bunting, flags, a damn good cocktail party and a first-class marching band, please write, well in advance, to the First Sea Lord, The Royal Navy, Whitehall, London SW1.

- If you are interested in joining the Army and wish to be underpaid, have premature arthritis, put your wife and family in a condemned hut miles from civilisation and are prepared to work your balls off day and night while watching the Treasury eroding your original terms and conditions and pension, serving mainly in sandy climes where you can't even get a drink; then please stay on the line. Your call will shortly be passed on to a bitter, passed-over recruiting sergeant in a grotty little office next to Lidl on the high street.

Have a nice day and thank you again for trying to contact The British Army.

A young, freshly minted lieutenant was sent to Bosnia as part of the peace-keeping mission. During a briefing on land mines, the captain asked for questions.

Our intrepid solder raised his hand and asked, "If we do happen to step on a mine, sir, what do we do?"

"Normal procedure, lieutenant, is to jump 200 feet in the air and scatter oneself over a wide area."

Q: How many military information officers does it take to change a light bulb?

A: At the present point in time it is against policy and the best interests of military strategy to divulge information of such a statistical nature. Next question, please.

After being briefed before their posting to Afghanistan, the major asked if the men had any questions. One young crow was brave enough to put up his hand and asked how he could tell the difference between a friendly Afghan and the Taliban.

The major smiled and told him that if he saw someone who looked suspicious he should call out, "Osama was a dickhead!" and if he was a member of the Taliban, he would shoot at you. Several months later, while touring the hospital, the major found the soldier in a bad way.

When asked what happened, the soldier replied, "I was doing what you told me... saw someone while on patrol and called to him, 'Osama was a dickhead.' He called back, 'David Cameron's a complete tosser!' and while we were in the middle of the road shaking hands, a truck ran us over!"

It is 5 o'clock in the morning at the training camp, well below freezing, and the soldiers are asleep in their barracks. The drill sergeant walks in and bellows, "THIS IS A BIRTHDAY SUIT INSPECTION! I want to see you all formed up outside butt-naked at the double!"

The soldiers quickly jump out of bed, naked and shivering, and run outside to form in their three ranks. The sergeant walks out and yells, "Close up the ranks, conserve your body heat!" So they close in slightly…

The captain comes along with his swagger stick. He goes to the first soldier and whacks him right across the chest with it.

"DID THAT HURT?" he yells.

"No, sir!" comes the reply.

"Why not?"

"Because I'm a Royal Green Jacket, sir!"

The captain is impressed, and walks on to the next man. He takes the stick and whacks the soldier right across the rear.

"Did THAT hurt?"

"No, sir!"

"Why not?"

"Because I'm a Royal Green Jacket, sir!"

Still extremely impressed, the captain walks to the third soldier, and notices he has an enormous erection. Naturally, he gives his target a huge whack with the swagger stick.

"Did THAT hurt?"

"No, sir!"

"Why not?"

"Because it belongs to the bloke behind me, sir!"

A fleeing insurgent, desperate for water, was plodding through the desert when he saw something far off in the distance. Hoping to find water, he hurried towards the oasis, only to find a gunner selling regimental ties. The insurgent asked, "Do you have water?" The gunner replied, "There is no water, the well is dry. Would you like to buy a tie instead? They are only five dinar."

The insurgent shouted, "You idiot! I do not need an over-priced tie. I need water! I should kill you, but I must find water first!"

"OK," said the gunner. "It does not matter that you do not want to buy a tie and that you hate me. I will show you that I am bigger than that. If you continue over that hill to the east for about two miles, you will find our officers' mess. It has all the ice-cold water you need."

Cursing, the insurgent staggered away over the hill. Several hours later he staggered back, collapsed with dehydration and gasped, "They won't let me in without a fucking tie."

A British army doctor is doing her rounds at Camp Bastion Military Hospital in Helmand Province. Having diligently taken the pulse of one poor fellow, she goes to record the heart rate on the patient's notes. Reaching behind her ear she is shocked to retrieve a thermometer. "Oh shit!" she curses. "One of the assholes in the last room must have my pen!"

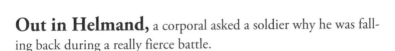

Out in Helmand, a corporal asked a soldier why he was falling back during a really fierce battle.

"Didn't you hear me say that we're outnumbered four to one?"

The private replied, "Well, I got my four, sir."

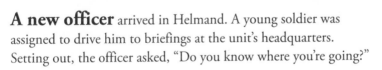

I'm being posted to the most dangerous spot in the world. It's somewhere between that Iraq/Kandahar place.

A new officer arrived in Helmand. A young soldier was assigned to drive him to briefings at the unit's headquarters. Setting out, the officer asked, "Do you know where you're going?"

The driver assured him that he did. But soon he pulled over to look at a map.

"Sergeant," the officer repeated, "do you know where you're going?"

"I know where I'm going, sir," he replied. "I just don't know how to get there from here."

Her Majesty the Queen is visiting troops in a military hospital in Iraq.

At the first bed she asks the soldier about his injuries.

"Well, ma'am," replies the soldier, "I received shrapnel wounds to my penis in a land mine explosion."

"How terrible," the Queen replies. "How are they treating you and what are your hopes for the future?"

"Well," replies the solider, "everyday they scrub my wounds with Dettol and a wire brush. When I'm well, I want to go back and fight for Queen and country."

At the second bed, the Queen again asks the soldier about his injuries.

"Well, Your Majesty," replies the soldier, "I was driving a tank which was targeted in a missile attack. When the fuel tank exploded I received terrible burns to my buttocks and anus and now have MRSA in my wounds."

"How are they treating you, and what are your plans for the future?" replies the Queen.

"Well, ma'am, they scrub my wounds daily with Dettol and a wire brush, and when I am well I will continue to fight for Queen and country."

Moving to the third bed, the Queen sees a soldier with a bandage wrapped around his jaw. "Well," asks the Queen, "what has happened to you?"

The shy soldier replies, "Well, ma'am, I feel somewhat of a fraud, but while on service I developed an impacted wisdom tooth, which in turn has formed an abscess that has become infected."

"Oh," replies the Queen. "And how are they treating you, and what do you hope for the future?"

The soldier bravely replies, "Well, ma'am, they are going to brush my teeth with Dettol, so my only hope for the future is that I use the wire brush before those other two bastards."

A paratrooper is describing his day to a friend. "In the air by 04:00 hours," he begins. "When we reached 20,000 feet, I jumped, deploying the canopy ten seconds after reaching terminal velocity. I landed three-clicks north of intended targets. After a 15-mile hike we engaged the enemy and after a short fire-fight killed all targets.

"We then negotiated the mined path back despite coming under friendly fire from our Yank friends and reached the pick-up point at 22:50 hours. After a couple of hours the choppers arrived and we were able to return to base."

"Bloody hell. That's some day," comments his friend.

"Nah!" replies the paratrooper. "Just what we call 'Normal-Para' activity."

1992. The US General Norman Schwarzkopf and the British General Sir Peter de la Billière were taking a well-earned break and discussing bravery.

Stormin' Norman said, "I'll show you American bravery." He called a big USMC sergeant over to him. He ordered him to climb to the top of a 50-foot tree that was outside the base, jump off and land on his head. Amazingly the Yank did exactly that. The American general turned to the Brit and said, "There! That's American bravery for you!"

General de la Billière said, "Let me show you British bravery." He then called a Royal Marine sergeant over and repeated, word for word, the US general's request. The marine turned around to face the British general and with a steely look in his eye said, "Go and fuck yourself, sir!"

De la Billière smiled and turned to the American general, saying, "Now that's British bravery for you – and brains to boot!"

An RAF major was showing off the new technologies on his reconnaissance aircraft. The clearly interested colonel stopped at one monitor and asked what it did.

"That's a chat screen, sir," said the attendant Aircraftman. "We use it to relay information to the crew – enemy positions etc. It's kind of like instant messaging, sir."

Impressed, the colonel continued his tour.

"Ah," he said, spotting a similar monitor. He tapped the airman's shoulder and nodded at the screen, "You seem to have a message." Before the poor man could do anything, up came the 'intelligence' warning: "Heads up! The Colonel is on his way!"

While practising auto-rotations during a military night-training exercise, an Apache screwed up the landing and landed on the tail rotor. The landing was so brutal it broke off the tail boom. However, the chopper remained upright on its skids, sliding down the runway doing 360s.

As the Apache slid past the tower, trailing a brilliant shower of sparks, the control tower attempted to make contact calling, "Sir, it's Tower. Do you require any assistance?"

The Apache answered, "Not sure, Tower, we haven't finished crashing yet!"

An Englishman, an Irishman, and a Scotsman are trying to enlist during the Gulf War. The sergeant major says to the Englishman. "OK, you're in the middle of the desert in an army jeep, enemy aircraft are coming at you firing bullets and dropping bombs. What are you going to do?"

The Englishman says, "I'd stop the jeep, get out and run."

"No good," says the sergeant major. "You're in the middle of nowhere with no cover. You would be killed. I'm afraid you've failed."

He then asks the Scotsman the same question. The Scotsman says, "I would stop the jeep and get under it."

"No good," barks the sergeant major again. "If a stray bullet or bomb hits the jeep, you're dead. You've failed."

He turns to the Irishman. "OK. You're in the middle of the desert in an army jeep, enemy aircraft coming at you, firing and dropping bombs. What are you going to do?" The Irishman replies, "I'd indicate left and turn right."

"Umm Qasr – a port in Iraq – is a city similar to Southampton," UK ex-Defence Minister Geoff Hoon said in the House of Commons. A British squaddie back from patrolling Umm Qasr responded by saying, "He's either never been to Southampton, or he's never been to Umm Qasr." His mate added, "There's no beer, no prostitutes and people are shooting at us. It's more like Portsmouth."

An insurgent officer was leading his squad through the desert when they came upon a large sand dune.

From the other side of the dune a voice called out, "One Royal Marine is better than ten insurgent soldiers!"

The officer signalled for ten of his men to assault the dune. There was gunfire and screams, followed by silence.

Then the mysterious voice called, "One Royal Marine is better than 100 insurgent troops!"

So the officer sent 100 men over the top. Again, there was a fierce exchange of fire, then silence.

The voice then chided, "One Royal Marine is better than 1000 insurgent soldiers!"

This time the enraged general signalled a whole battalion to charge the dune. A major battle ensued, there was shooting and shouting for almost an hour. Then silence.

A single insurgent soldier crawled over the crest of the dune, bloodied and battered, and said, "Sir, don't send any more men, it's a trap...there are two Royal Marines."

An American army camp in Iraq hung a home-made sign outside their barracks, it read:
'Second To None'.

The British troops then put up their own sign:
'None'.

An English army major gave a speech to a group of newly graduating Afghan soldiers. To lighten the tone he told his favourite joke – a rambling shaggy-dog story that took a few minutes to tell. His interpreter then quickly translated the joke, using only seven or eight words. Everyone immediately burst into hearty laughter. The major continued his talk, but when he had finished he asked the interpreter how he had been able to retell such a relatively long joke so quickly.

"Well, sir," the Afghan interpreter replied. "I didn't think everyone would get the point, so I said, 'the major has just told a joke. Everyone please laugh.'"

The captain called the padre in for a quiet word. "Your church services always start five or ten minutes late, padre. This is the army, we do things punctually. When the general instructs us to leave camp at 05:30 hours, he doesn't mean 05:35 or 05:40."

The padre thought for a moment before replying, "Yes. But my general outranks your general."

"I suppose," snarled the vicious sergeant major to the private, "that when you're discharged from the army, you'll wait for me to die, just so you can spit on my grave."

"Not me," said the private. "When I get out of the army, I never want to join a queue again."

A wing commander was taking out a first-tour flight lieutenant as co-pilot on his first mission in the CH-46. The pilot said, "I will do all of the flying since this is your first combat mission. When we get into the zone, I will tell you to open the ramp. That is so the Pongos can run out the back. After we lift out of the zone, I will tell you to close the ramp. That is all you have to do on this mission. Do you understand?"

"Yes, sir!" replied the flight lieutenant.

The CH-46 was loaded with the battle group and the pilot took off for the LZ. As the pilot flew down into the zone, the helicopter started taking fire from automatic weapons. Eager to get his men into the fray he shouted, "Lower the ramp!" But when he looked over, the co-pilot was just sitting there gazing into space.

The pilot reached up and hit the ramp toggle switch to the 'open' position. When the last soldier had jumped off the ramp, the pilot shouted over the intercom, "Close the ramp!" But when he looked over the co-pilot was still just sitting there looking straight ahead. So he quickly reached over and closed the ramp.

Several minutes later when heading for Sangin, the pilot said, "I gave you only two things to do on this operation and you didn't do either one of them. I want to know why in the hell you didn't obey my commands back there!"

The co-pilot peered over at the pilot and said, "Do I bother you when you're taking a shit?"

A famous TV war reporter was embedded with troops on patrol in Helmand. After witnessing a particularly vicious fire-fight, he interviewed one member of an elite sniper team. Milking the interview for all it was worth, he asked the young soldier in a less than respectful tone, "What do you feel, if anything, when you cold-bloodedly shoot an Afghan fighter from such a long distance?"

The young soldier shrugged his shoulders and replied, "Recoil?"

During the heightening of tension over the Falkland Islands, Argentina banned ships flying the British ensign from docking in their ports. One of the first boats to test the blockade was a Royal Navy patrol boat. An Argentine destroyer came alongside and hoisted a signal ordering them to stop. The patrol boat ignored it, so the destroyer hoisted another signal saying if the patrol continued they would fire a warning shot across its bow.

The navy skipper turned to the signalman and told him to hoist another signal that read "THFFZZ!"

"Let's see them find that in the code book," he said.

"Yes, sir," replied the signalman. "But what does it mean?"

"It's the nearest I can get to a raspberry," replied the captain.

HOW TO PREPARE FOR A DEPLOYMENT TO AFGHANISTAN

1. Sleep on a camp bed in the garage.
2. Replace the garage door with a curtain.
3. Six hours after you go to sleep, have your wife or girlfriend whip open the curtain, shine a flashlight in your eyes and mumble, "Sorry, wrong cot."
4. Renovate your bathroom. Hang a green plastic sheet down from the middle of your bath and move the showerhead down to chest level. Keep four inches of soapy cold water on the floor. Stop cleaning the toilet and pee everywhere but in the toilet itself. Leave two to three sheets of toilet paper.
5. When you take a shower, wear flip-flops and keep the lights off.
6. Every time there is a thunderstorm, go sit in a wobbly rocking chair and dump dirt on your head.
7. Put lube oil in a humidifier instead of water and set it on 'HIGH' for that tactical generator smell.
8. Don't watch TV except for movies in the middle of the night. Have your family vote on which movie to watch and then show a different one.
9. Leave a lawnmower running in your living room 24 hours a day for a proper noise level.
10. Get a drunk tramp to give you a haircut.
11. Make up your family food menu a week ahead of time without looking in your food cabinets or refrigerator. Then serve some kind of meat in an unidentifiable sauce poured over noodles. Do this for every meal.
12. Go out for long pointless walks, talking to various people you encounter. Repeat what you have to say to each of them a dozen times – each time speaking ever more slowly.
13. Sit in your car and let it run for four hours with the windows down before going anywhere. Tune the radio to static and monitor it.
14. When your child asks for a sweet, make him find the exact sweet he wants on the internet and print out the web page. Type up a form and staple the web page to the back. Submit the paperwork to your spouse for processing. After two weeks, give your child the sweet.
15. Set your alarm clock to go off at random times during the night. When it goes off, jump out of bed and get to the shower as fast as you can. Make sure that the shower temperature is set to cold.
16. Once a month, take every major appliance completely apart and put it back together again.

17. Use 18 scoops of coffee per pot and allow it to sit for five to six hours before drinking.
18. Invite at least 185 people you don't really like because of their strange hygiene habits to come and visit for a couple of months. Exchange clothes with them.
19. Have a fluorescent lamp installed on the bottom of your coffee table and lie under it to read books.
20. Raise the thresholds and lower the top sills of your front and back doors so that you either trip over the threshold or hit your head on the sill every time you pass through one of them.
21. Keep a roll of toilet paper by your bed and bring it to the bathroom with you along with your gun and a flashlight.
22. Go to the bathroom when you just have to pass wind, "just in case". Every time.
23. Announce to your family that they have some post. Get them to report to you after supper and then say, "Sorry, it's not for you after all."
24. Wash only 15 items of laundry per week. Roll up the semi-wet clean clothes in a ball. Place them in a cloth sack in the corner of the garage where the cat pees. After a week, unroll and wear them without ironing or removing the mildew.
25. Go to the worst crime-infested place you can find, heavily armed, wearing a flak jacket and a Kevlar helmet. Set up a tent in a car park, call the local residents over and announce that you are there to help them.
26. Eat a single M&M every Sunday and convince yourself it will stop you getting malaria.
27. Demand each family member be limited to ten minutes per week for one morale-lifting phone call.
28. Shoot a few bullet holes in the walls of your home for proper ambience.
29. Sandbag the floor of your car to protect from mine blasts and fragmentation.
30. While driving down roads in your car, stop at each crossroads and drain and inspect them for remotely detonated explosives before proceeding.
31. Let off 50 fireworks simultaneously in your driveway at three in the morning. When startled neighbours appear, tell them all is well, you are just registering mortars. Tell them plastic will make an acceptable substitute for their shattered windows.
32. Wait for the coldest day of the year and announce to your family that there will be no heating that day so you can perform much-needed maintenance on the boiler.
33. Just when you think you're ready to resume a normal life, order yourself to repeat this process for another six months.

Paul is in a military hospital after receiving injuries from a mortar attack. He wakes to find his best mate Danny sitting by him.

"Hey, Dan, back again, mate? You were there when I got hit, weren't you?"

"Yeah, I brought you in," nods Danny. "Thought I'd better check that you were OK."

Paul raises himself in his bed. "You've always been there for me. I remember you looked after me when I got hit by that sniper in Iraq."

"I did, mate," replied his friend.

"And you were there by my side in that tank attack back in Bosnia."

"I was indeed, mate. That was severe. But that's what friends are for."

Paul sat up a little further, looked at his mate and said, "I'm beginning to think you're a fucking jinx!"

SOD'S LAW

- All five-second grenade fuses will burn down in three seconds.

- Things that must be together to work usually can't be shipped together.

- Radios will fail as soon as you are desperate for fire support.

- Anything you do can get you shot – including doing nothing.

- The only thing more accurate than incoming fire is incoming friendly fire.

- When both sides are convinced that they are about to lose, they are right.

- The easy way out is always mined.

- A bullet with your name on it will always get you. So will the ones addressed 'To Whom It May Concern'.

- Body armour only protects the parts the bullets miss.

- Combat will occur on the ground between two adjoining maps.

- The further you fly from base, the louder the strange engine noises become.

BULLETIN BOARD NOTICE:

The following men will pick up their Good Conduct medals at the Admin Office this afternoon. Failure to comply with this order will result in disciplinary action.

CIVVY STREET

A junior officer at the Ministry of Defence was a hard worker, and he had a very nice well-furnished office. However, he began behaving strangely. First he shoved his desk out into the space also occupied by his secretary's desk. Then a few days later, as he was leaving for the day, he pushed his desk out into one of the many long corridors. He worked there for a few days, and then he shoved his desk into the men's toilet and set up work there.

All of this had not escaped the notice of his fellow workers. It seemed more and more strange to them, so strange that they did not dare ask the officer himself what he was doing. Instead, they went to the division psychiatrist and asked him to examine the officer.

So the psychiatrist walked into the men's toilet, sat on the edge of the officer's desk and asked, "Why have you kept moving your desk? And why into the men's lavatory?"

"Well," said the officer, "this seems to be the only place in the MOD where they know what they're doing."

A company hired a new employee. He was smart and very good at his job, but his punctuality was very poor. By the end of the first month he was coming into work an hour late each day. The boss decided to have words. The man shrugged his shoulders and agreed he came in late.

"What time would you get in your last job?" asked the boss.

"Just the same. I'd get up, have a leisurely breakfast, read the papers and eventually make my way to the office."

"And what did they say there when you walked in?" asked the CEO incredulously.

The employee thought for a second. "They'd usually say, 'Good morning, Air Vice-Marshal'."

A man was being interviewed for a job.

"Were you in the service?" ask the interviewer.

"Yes, I was a soldier," responded the applicant.

"Did you see any active duty?"

"I served in Iraq, sir, and I'm afraid as a result I have a partial disability."

"May I ask what happened?"

"Well, I had a grenade go off between my legs and I lost both testicles."

"You're hired. You can start Monday at ten a.m."

"I thought work started at nine? I don't want any preferential treatment because of my disability."

"Everyone else starts at nine a.m. but, to be honest, nothing gets done between nine and ten. We just sit around for an hour scratching our balls."

"Last night I saw the film *War Games.*"

"Any good?"

"Well, it's about a computer hacker who nearly starts World War Three when he and his girlfriend break into America's military defence system."

"Yeah, that's a bit far-fetched, a computer hacker with a girlfriend!"

A Scotsman in a Middle East bar sees a man with a black beard buy a bottle of beer from the barman. He drinks it and turns to leave.

The barman says, "Hey, aren't you going to pay?"

The man says, "SAS," and winks at him.

A little later another bearded man comes in, orders a beer, downs it and, rubbing his beard, nods to the barman.

The barman nods back, and the guy leaves.

The Scotsman thinks, "I'll have some of that," so he goes to the bar and gets another couple of whiskies.

When he turns to leave, again the barman says, "Hey, aren't you going to pay?"

So the Scotsman says, "SAS," and winks at him.

But then the barman asks, "Where's your beard?"

Thinking quickly, the Scotsman lifts his kilt and says, "Secret service."

Fearing that young people are failing to get the message of how vulnerable Britain is to terrorist attack, MI5 have now produced recoded levels of terror threat that can be understood by everyone:

OMFG! .... An attack is expected imminently.

OMG! .... An attack is highly likely.

WTF? .... An attack is possible; awaiting confirmation.

LOL .... Means an attack is unlikely.

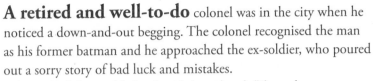

A retired and well-to-do colonel was in the city when he noticed a down-and-out begging. The colonel recognised the man as his former batman and he approached the ex-soldier, who poured out a sorry story of bad luck and mistakes.

"Now look here, old chap" said the colonel. "I've a decent country pile and need some help around the house and that sort of stuff. We'll get you cleaned up and you can start right away."

The old soldier was duly grateful but asked how he might serve his old colonel. "You can start off as though you were my batman, as in the old days, and just do exactly as you did then," replied the colonel.

The following morning at 07:00 sharp, there was a tap on the colonel's bedroom door. In came the old soldier with a cup of tea. He opened the curtains, placed the tea beside the colonel and wished him a good morning, with a brief word about the weather. He then went to the other side of the bed, pulled back the covers, smacked the colonel's wife smartly across the bottom and said, "It's back to the village with you, my girl!"

A big bloke spilled my pint in the pub, so I shouted at him, "Look what you've done! You've spilt my pint!"

"Before you start, mate, I spent three years in the Paras, two years in the SAS, a year in the Foreign Legion and the last year teaching unarmed combat, so what does that tell you?"

"That you can't stick at anything?" I replied.

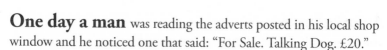

One day a man was reading the adverts posted in his local shop window and he noticed one that said: "For Sale. Talking Dog. £20."

The man noticed that the address was nearby, so he decided to call round and check it out.

"Hello," he said when a man opened the door. "I saw your ad about the dog. But surely there's some mistake."

"No. There's no mistake," replied the seller.

"Not a mistake? You mean you actually have a talking dog?"

"Yes, see for yourself. He's in the lounge."

The man walks into the lounge, and sees a dog sitting on the sofa, his paws behind his head.

Slightly embarrassed, he mutters: "Erm… are you the talking dog?"

The dog turns and looks at him, and says, "Yes. Nice to meet you."

The man is stunned. "Where did you learn to speak English," he asks.

The dog replies, "Well, it started in the RAF. I used to be a dog instructor at the Ministry of Aircraft Production Guard Dog School in Gloucester. I started learning English there. Then I was transferred to Army Special Forces. I went on missions in Latin America, my English improved and I even picked up a little Spanish. After that, I was transferred to the SAS, where I went undercover in Africa. I learned some French and a smattering of Eritrean while I was doing that. Before I retired, I was transferred to the Royal Navy, where I was a K-9 dog in Italy. I just couldn't help adding some Italian to my repertoire…"

The man was absolutely gobsmacked. He went back to the seller and said, "That's completely amazing. How can you sell a dog like that for £20?"

The man replied, "Because he's a bloody liar. He never even joined the Armed Forces…"

A young man gets on a bus one day and, as usual, looks around to find it full of old people. He's used to the vague smell of damp clothes and urine, but the bloke next to him jerks his head to one side every few moments in a really irritating way.

"Can't you sit still?" says the young bloke. "What on earth is wrong with you?"

The old fella replies. "Hey, sonny, don't be so rude. It's a nervous tic I suffered from being in the trenches during the war."

Soon the old timer gets off and another old chap takes his place. He is just as annoying, his uncontrollable spasms causing his leg to kick out, often in the man's direction.

"I'm so sorry," explains the old man. "It's an affliction I developed during the war. My ship was bombed in the middle of the Atlantic."

The young bloke sighs and goes back to looking out of the window. By time he looks round another old guy is sitting next to him. The youngster waits to discover what is up with him and, sure enough, this one starts madly flicking his hand around.

"Let me guess," begins the young man sardonically. "You picked that up in the War?"

"No," replies the old bloke. "I picked it out of my nose. But I can't get it off my hand."

Out in Afghanistan, three soldiers – an American, an Englishman and an Irishman – have been captured by the Taliban. At first they are told that they will be shot at dawn but, after some whispering and arguing, the mullah tells them that as it is a special festival day, they will have the chance to be released. Their freedom will depend on whether they could sing a song which mentions a dog.

The American says, "That's easy, I'm a big Elvis fan and I've always loved to sing 'You Ain't Nothing but a Hound Dog'.

"Fine," said the mullah, and the American is set free.

The Englishman then says, "I remember one from my childhood," and started singing, 'How Much is That Doggy in the Window'.

"That will do," says the disappointed Taliban, and the Englishman is released.

The Irishman smiles and says, "I'm afraid you're going to have to let me go as well, gentleman. Listen to this," and he begins to sing Sinatra's 'Strangers in the Night'.

"'Strangers in the Night'?" asked the mullah. "Where's the dog in that?"

"You didn't let me get to the chorus," replied Paddy. "Scooby do be-do-be-doo!"